FALLING TO HEAVEN

FALLING TO HEAVEN

*The Surprising Path
to Happiness*

JAMES L. FERRELL

DESERET
BOOK

SALT LAKE CITY, UTAH

DESERET BOOK is a registered trademark of Deseret Book Company.

Visit us at DeseretBook.com

Library of Congress Cataloging-in-Publication Data

(CIP on file)
ISBN 978-1-60908-900-9

Printed in the United States of America
Publishers Printing, Salt Lake City, UT

10   9   8   7   6   5   4   3   2   1

"The Lord upholdeth all that fall, and raiseth up all those that be bowed down."

—Psalm 145:14

CONTENTS

CONTENTS

INTRODUCTION

In a church meeting I once attended, a visiting speaker opened his remarks with the following question: "Do you think Jesus loved himself? Of course he did!" he insisted enthusiastically, responding to his own question. "How else could he love others so much if he didn't first love himself?"

Over the years since, I have been on the lookout for scriptural support for this idea. In all that time, I have yet to find a single verse of scripture that speaks of Jesus' self-love. Countless scriptures tell us that he loves his Father and loves us. Indeed, those two themes are apparently among the most important in all the scripture. But that he loves *himself?* Not even a whisper. It seems that the topic didn't interest him.

Although I have never heard another person in the Church

even mention the issue of Jesus' self-love, I hear a lot of talk about whether we love *ourselves*—whether we feel good about ourselves, for example, or whether we can forgive ourselves, or accept ourselves. I have wondered whether it is wise and helpful for those who are commanded to follow Jesus in all things to expend our energies trying to secure a self-regard and self-worth that the Lord appears never to have valued. The scripture sometimes cited in favor of such efforts—the commandment to love our neighbors as ourselves[1]—has increasingly become inverted in our modern age to mean that we must love ourselves so that we can love our neighbors. But is this really what Jesus was teaching?

My understanding of this commandment is that we are to feel just as happy for another's good fortune as we would for our own. It is a description of the kind of love that bound Jonathan to David, even though David would supplant Jonathan, King Saul's heir, from the throne. Whereas envious Saul spent the last decade of his life trying to kill the one who would take the scepter from his house, humble Jonathan symbolically transferred his own kingly raiment to David— loving him, the scriptures say, "as his own soul."[2] Who can read that epic story of friendship and declare in summary, "My, how he must have loved himself!" No, from that story, and from the commandment that memorializes the love it describes, we learn that to love another as oneself is to have our souls so "knit together in unity and in love"[3] that we make no distinctions between ourselves and others in our hearts. We rejoice with others in their successes and join with them in their sorrows. As Paul wrote, we "remember them that are in bonds, as bound with them; and them which suffer adversity, as being [ourselves]."[4] This, I believe, is the kind of love Jesus was talking about, which is worlds apart from the idea of an indulgent love of self.

Notwithstanding this, when we feel down, the world urges us to try to feel "up"—to stop being too hard on ourselves, to dwell upon our strengths, and to forgive and love ourselves. By contrast, the scriptures specifically condemn those who become "lovers of their own selves."[5] *Don't seek to find yourself,* Jesus famously warned.[6] Rather, "preach naught but repentance."[7] "Come unto me [and] I will show unto [you your] weakness."[8]

Whether we are feeling up or feeling down, the scriptures suggest that the path of rescue lies in the one direction our natural-man[9] tendencies keep us from looking. As absurd as it may sound, happiness apparently lies not in our trying to feel better about ourselves but rather through our allowing the Lord to help us see truths that at first might make us feel worse. In these lowest moments—the moments when we give up resisting what we haven't wanted to see—we are finally immersed in the joy we have always sought but have never found, a joy that comes not because we have lifted our hearts but because we have finally allowed them to break.

Perhaps, like me, you have sometimes felt "stuck"—unfulfilled, for example, or complacent, or unhappy, and unable to find a way out of your struggle. Or perhaps you have felt flawed, or forgotten, or unfairly burdened. Maybe you grieve as you find your faith at times waning, or your desire to do good diminishing. Maybe you have concluded that even God can't save you.

Whatever our struggles, a great truth at the heart of the gospel reveals a most surprising path to happiness. The path is always right before us, but it begins in the one place our burdened or complacent hearts are keeping us from looking. Happiness, like heaven, may seem above us, but it turns out that we don't obtain either of them by climbing.

PART ONE

A SURPRISING TRUTH

1

MAKING SENSE OF HAPPINESS

A man I'll call Jeff Watson stared blankly at his computer screen. The curtains to his home office were drawn tightly shut, the darkened, hemmed-in room mirroring his soul. His wife of eighteen years had taken the children to her parents' home for the weekend. He was alone. Terribly and frighteningly alone.

They had finally had the talk he had long run from—the exchange in which divorce was not only raised as a possibility but the preliminary planning had begun. Who would have the kids? She wanted them. So did he. In the cool arithmetic of those trying to bridle firestorms of emotion, they agreed that they would let the kids choose, off-loading that heart-aching choice to the only people in the family who didn't deserve to have to make it. Jeff wanted desperately to believe that it was a scene from another person's life. But it wasn't. This was his life, and everything he cared about was collapsing all around him.

Jeff confided in me after a sleepless, tear-filled night. His soul struggled so desperately for sustaining breath that he could barely squeeze in words between his heavings. At first, I thought he was gravely ill. "No, Jim," he choked, "it's not that. It's—" And then my friend started bawling. I had never heard pain like I heard in his anguished, sobbing cries. After my multiple attempts to try to get him to tell me what was wrong, he finally was able to say, "Tammy's left me, Jim. It's over. Everything—everything's over." And then the wave of sorrow overcame him again.

I sat in stunned silence, my mind racing to understand what I had just heard. The Jeff and Tammy Watsons of this world don't get divorced. Those of us who were privileged to know them had hope in our own marriages partly because of what we saw in theirs. What I was hearing was impossible.

But sometimes the impossible is what's most true, even when it's heartbreaking. I listened as Jeff talked about years spent in secret struggle. What a lonely and difficult thing to suffer in such an outwardly happy way! He spoke of the burden he had long carried of living a hypocritical life, of not loving as he had long preached that we should love, of growing in bitterness even as he professed to forgive. He spoke of the foreboding future he now saw: rumors, innuendo, a release from his Church calling, a possible end to his career. He could barely speak about his children and what this might do to them. "Where did I go wrong?" he pleaded, more to the universe than to me in particular. "What have I done to deserve this?"

With these thoughts, the sorrow in his voice turned to anger. He was angry at his wife, angry about his predicament—angry, alas, with God. And he was terrified by all of it.

In this heart-wrenching, pivotal moment, I didn't know what to say. Everything I could think of sounded trite. So I just listened. He thanked me for my understanding ear, but the truth was, I didn't know what else to offer him.

I've thought about this experience over the years since. The Lord might have stopped me from speaking that morning, knowing from his divine perspective that it was not the moment for counsel. Or perhaps I was simply unprepared to be the tool in the Lord's hands that I otherwise could have been. Whichever the case, the blank I drew in the face of Jeff's heartache caused me to question my own understanding of the anatomy of happiness. If I was speechless about his predicament, I was very likely lost concerning my own as well. More earnestly, I began to ponder the following question: When we are struggling, where is happiness actually to be found?

What I have learned in response to this question has been one of the biggest surprises of my life. It turns out that when

I am unhappy, almost all my intuitions about happiness lead me astray. The promising path is routinely the one I'm not taking—in fact, the one I would never consider taking because it seems from my unhappy place to be absurdly and obviously wrong. Let me give an example of this from the scriptures.

> Come unto me, all ye that labour and are heavy laden [Jesus invited], and I will give you rest.[10]

So far so good. I certainly want the Lord to relieve me of my burdens and give me rest. But then Jesus introduced the way that our burdens can be lifted, and this is where the surprises begin. For he teaches that our burdens are lifted only as we take upon ourselves an additional burden!

> Take my yoke upon you . . . and ye shall find rest unto your souls. For my yoke is easy and my burden is light.[11]

Think about what this means. When we are feeling burdened, weighed down, and heavy, Jesus is telling us that relief comes only as we do what all of our intuitions tell us is the *last* thing we should do—take upon ourselves an additional burden. Although yokes distribute burdens between partners, Jesus is asking us to take on the burden of a yoke we aren't presently carrying. This is an *additional* weight, or at least it seems to be, and therefore what sounds like an added measure of heaviness.

This particular weight, it turns out, is different from all others. It is a weight that lifts, a burden that is light, a heaviness that brings peace to the soul. Which, of course, sounds absurd. So the world, with all good intentions, looks for happiness in other ways—embarking on paths that seem, by their very natures, more happy and promising. As I have walked my own share of such paths, I have learned that what they offer is a mirage—a kind of cotton candy to the soul that leaves us emptier or else more puffed up than before.

So where does this leave us? As I have studied and pondered upon this question, I have been awakened to an incredibly helpful idea—a great truth that Jesus and all of his prophets have freely taught but that I had nevertheless been missing: Happiness so often seems elusive because it rests on a paradox—an apparent contradiction that lies at the very heart of the gospel. This book is an attempt to bring out into the open the liberating paradox that is at the center of our beliefs. It is a book about happiness, and the surprising way it is found.

I believe that you will find this to be both an easy and a challenging book. I think you will find it easy to read—interesting, surprising, hopefully even engaging. But if you are like me, you will also find it difficult, at times, to put into practice. And the reason for this is precisely because happiness rests on believing Jesus even when what he is telling us seems mistaken. *Come take this burden, that you may be light,*[12] he tells us. *Lose yourself that you may find.*[13] I believe we will discover together that no words of Jesus are more important than those that don't seem to make sense, and that we will find great and surprising relief in this discovery.

Paradoxes can seem difficult to penetrate at first, precisely because they seem like they can't be true. The divine paradox will seem this way as well, so we need to lay the groundwork for it carefully, so that we will understand both what is at stake and the liberating happiness that it makes possible. I would just ask that you not depart from this journey together before the payoff comes. Through Parts 1 and 2 of this book, we will explore the doctrine of the divine paradox. In Part 3 we will explore its practical implications, and then in Part 4 we will discover the surprising way that happiness is found. As with any journey, the last half can be reached only by walking the earlier half of the trail. Hang in there. Enjoy the stroll. What at first may seem like a burden will end up being easy and light and will bring rest to the soul.[14]

We will start on our journey at the beginning—by discussing first what a paradox is, and then by naming the great paradox from which happiness flows.

2

TRUTH IN
CONTRADICTION

I once saw a T-shirt with this message on the front: "The sentence on the back of this shirt is true." Then, on the back, it said this: "The sentence on the front of this shirt is a lie." The two statements make the mind spin, don't they? That's because they form a paradox—a self-contradictory and therefore absurd statement. The paradox at the heart of the gospel is not like this one. The divine paradox *seems* to be a contradiction, but it actually expresses the deepest and most exquisite truth. The trouble is, since it seems like a contradiction, we can easily resist or dismiss it. If we do, we miss all that it offers, including an understanding of happiness.

Sometimes I find it helpful to think by analogy, and regarding paradoxes, some of the clearest examples are from sports.

For example, consider weight training. How do we build our muscles up? By breaking them down. That seems paradoxical, doesn't it? But it's nevertheless how it works.

Similarly, think about rebounding a basketball. The natural reflex when rebounding is to go to the hoop to get the ball. But this is a mistake. The best rebounders don't move *toward* the basket to get the ball, they move *away*. That is, their first move is to step away from the basket to seal off their opponents. This is hard to do because it seems backwards. To put it in scriptural voice, "Move to the ball and you will miss it; move away and ye shall find."

Or consider biking. When I first started road biking, every day I tried to ride as fast as I could. It seemed obvious that the way to build strength and be able to ride faster was always to pedal as hard as possible. But then I met a wise man and master cyclist, and I learned this paradoxical truth: "If you want to go fast, you have to go slow." *What?* I responded. *That doesn't make sense!* But it does. The building of strength and speed requires regular rides of only moderate pace in order to build what riders call their "base." To put it scripturally, "To go fast, ye must needs go slow."

Similar paradoxes abound in golf. If you want to hit the ball hard, for example, it turns out that it usually helps to swing easy. And to hit the ball up, you have to swing down. Most of us who golf are hackers because in order to do it well you have to submit to the paradoxes that lie at the game's core. Our bodies resist. "I'm going to crush this ball!" we say to ourselves, and we tense up the very muscles that need to be relaxed in order to hit a good shot. Insisting on doing what seems natural and logical, we end up doing exactly the wrong thing!

The existence of an important *divine* paradox is implied by how often the Lord and his prophets speak in paradoxical terms. Jesus famously taught, "He that findeth his life shall lose it: and he that loseth his life for my sake shall find it."[15] To his disciples he said, "Whosoever of you will be the chiefest, shall be servant of all."[16] Concerning wisdom, Paul declared, "If any man among you seemeth to be wise in this world, let him become a fool, that he may be wise."[17] "When I am weak," he declared elsewhere, "then am I strong."[18]

Consider as well the paradoxical nature of the central elements of the gospel. *God* became *man*. Mankind *fell* so that they might become *exalted*. Jesus *died* so that we might *live*. Our "garments are made *white* in his *blood*."[19] "And with his *stripes* we are *healed*."[20]

"Compared to God," President Dieter F. Uchtdorf has said, "man is nothing; yet we are everything to God."[21] He called this the "paradox of man," and warned against concentrating only on one half of the paradox. We may think that happiness is found by focusing only on the happy second half of the statement, for example—on the reality of God's love. But this is a mistake. We cannot understand the infinite depth of God's love unless we can grasp the extent of our own nothingness before him, and we cannot understand our nothingness apart from the loving Being who saves us from it. The two parts are a whole, and the truth emerges from the apparent contradiction.

Considering these various examples, it seems that certain central truths of the gospel are most accurately expressed through paradox. If so, here is our challenge: Until we penetrate the divine paradox, we will reflexively resist it. It will seem strange to us, or mistaken, or difficult to understand or to implement. The temptation will be to give up and go back to our old ways—back to focusing on or doing what feels easier or more natural. But that would be a mistake. When we begin to tire of lifting weights, that's exactly when we need to keep doing it. When the basketball is lofting toward the hoop, that's precisely when we need to move away. When we are wondering whether God loves us, the answer may paradoxically lie in discovering, as Moses and the people of King Benjamin did, how we are less than we have ever before supposed![22]

So it seems that the pathways to the answers we seek are often exactly where we are not looking. This means that in order to put off the unhappiness of the natural man,[23] we must first do what feels *unnatural* to the natural man. And that requires that we to submit to, rather than resist, the paradox. Which, of course, is an act of faith, a reality that brings us to the mother of all paradoxes, the divine paradox that governs our ability to receive the blessings of the tree of life—the fruit of which, the prophet Lehi taught us, fills one's soul "with exceedingly great joy" and is "desirable to make one happy."[24]

3

THE DIVINE
PARADOX

In his remarkable vision,[25] the prophet Lehi describes five groups of people. Each successive group differs from the one before in a single way, and these single distinctions add up to the difference between personal stagnation and overflowing joy.

On one side of a river there rose a "great and spacious building," filled to the brim with those Lehi is careful to tell us were "both old and young, both male and female."[26] Clearly no people in any category were immune from putting themselves in this building. And what were they doing? They were mocking those who desired to partake of the fruit of the tree.[27]

These multitudes in the building[28] were divided from the rest by a "great and terrible gulf," which represented the "justice of the Eternal God."[29] A river ran along this gulf from the tree out to the river's head, beyond which was a "large and spacious field, as if it had been a world."[30] In this field we encounter the second group of people—"numberless concourses." Unlike those in the first group, these people were not in an attitude of mocking righteousness. As a result, they were not (at least not yet) divided from the righteous by the great gulf of justice.

We are then told of a third group—a subset of those in the field. "Many" of these people in the field, Lehi tells us, were "pressing forward that they might obtain the path which led unto the tree" of life.[31] They distinguished themselves from the second group by setting out after righteousness. They wanted to partake of the fruit of the tree. However, these people lost their way and wandered off the path when the way became obscured by "an exceedingly great mist of darkness,"[32] which represented the "temptations of the devil."[33]

A fourth group made it through the mist of darkness all the way to the tree. What was different about this group? In addition to setting out on the path, they "caught hold of" and "clung to" the rod of iron that paralleled it. This clinging to the rod (or word of God[34]) allowed them to press forward through those mists "even until they did come forth and partake of the fruit of the tree."[35] They made it! But, as you may know, they didn't stay. The scripture says that after they had partaken of the fruit "they did cast their eyes about as if they were ashamed."[36] They were ashamed, we are told, "because of those that were scoffing at them" from the great and spacious building across the gulf. They slunk away and fell into "forbidden paths and were lost."[37]

The question is, why? I believe that the answer to this question reveals the key to happiness itself—the key that unlocks the paradox of the fifth and final group:

> To be short in writing, Lehi saw other multitudes [like group 2] pressing forward [like group 3]; and they came and caught hold of the end of the rod of iron [like group 4]; and they did press their way forward, continually holding fast to the rod of iron [again, like group 4], until they came forth and fell down and partook of the fruit of the tree.[38]

Unlike group 4, this group stayed at the tree once they had obtained it. They were able to receive the happiness and joy that Lehi said resulted from the tree's fruit. The question is, how? What single thing did this group do that the prior group did not? If you read the above passage again, you may notice something odd near the end—something that doesn't make sense: a paradox. Think about trees, and fruit, and harvesting, and then read the passage again. Look for what doesn't make sense. Find the paradox.

Do you see it? Does the passage accurately describe how we normally harvest from trees? Don't we normally reach *up* to pick fruit? Then what are we to make of this group falling *down* to partake of the fruit, and of the fact that their falling down was the only thing that distinguished them from the group that fell away? As I've thought about those who fell away after reaching up for the fruit, it has occurred to me that their reaching up perhaps implies a level of pride that left them susceptible to the criticism and pride of the world. By contrast, the humility of those who found happiness by falling down rendered the pride of the world powerless.

So at the heart of the gospel we encounter a world-shifting, direction-obliterating paradox. In the gospel, it appears that up isn't up and down isn't down. After all, those who reached up fell, while those who fell were lifted. And the great and spacious building that was so "up" it "stood as it were in the air, high above the earth,"[39] ended up falling, "and the fall thereof," the scriptures emphasize, "was exceedingly great."[40]

Regarding happiness and joy, then, it appears that up may not be up and down may not be down. Rather, we begin to see the surprising outlines of a divine paradox. As nonsensical as it may at first sound, in the gospel, and regarding happiness, up appears to be down and down appears to be up.

And that, it seems to me, is a paradox worth pondering.

4

THE FALSE
DOCTRINE OF UP

C hapters 30 through 32 of the book of Alma combine to
form a fascinating exploration of the perils of thinking
that happiness depends on feeling up or good about oneself.
Approximately seventy-four years before Christ, the scripture
says that "there came a man into the land of Zarahemla, and
he was Anti-Christ, for he began to preach unto the people
against the prophecies . . . concerning the coming of Christ."[41]
This man, Korihor, traveled from city to city attempting to, in
his view, rescue the people from the oppression of their beliefs.
"O ye that are bound *down* under a foolish and a vain hope," he
boomed, "why do ye yoke yourself with such foolish things?"[42]
In essence, he admonished, "Don't bind yourselves *down* under
the foolish ordinances and performances laid down by ancient

priests."[43] Instead, he preached, we should "lift *up* our heads" and "look *up* with boldness."[44] "And thus he did preach unto [the people]," we are told, "leading away the hearts of many, causing them to lift *up* their heads in their wickedness."[45]

Notice all the "ups" and "downs" in those references. Korihor criticized the church on the basis that the practices and commandments of the church had the effect of making people feel bad. For one who believed that it is always bad to feel bad, this meant that the church was necessarily mistaken. His advice to those who were feeling burdened was to lighten their load by rejecting anything that felt like a burden. *Free yourself!* he urged them. *You're great! Being down is just a downer. Look up with boldness!* In this view, happiness is achieved by escaping the oppressions that would cause one to feel bad about oneself and instead focusing on—even glorying in—one's strengths.[46] *What depressing business it is to have to look to another for the remission of your sins,* he taught. He called it the effect of a "frenzied" and "deranged" mind.[47] *Don't hang your head down,* he told the people, *don't feel bad, and certainly don't feel guilty. That is no way to happiness.* His was a philosophy, "pleasing unto the carnal mind,"[48] that is repeated in many books one would find on the self-help shelves of our modern bookstores. And the people of his day, as well as ours, bought it. Alma tells us that this philosophy led away "many women, and also men."[49]

And yet, the end of this man verifies the truth not of his words but of the divine paradox that counters them. For this great believer in the happiness of "up" was "trodden *down*," we are told, "even until he was dead. And thus we see," the scripture concludes, "that the devil will not support his children at the last day, but doth speedily drag them *down* to hell."[50] The chief preacher of the doctrine of up was, by his efforts, dragged down to damnation.

It is a brutal irony that the people who killed Korihor were those who perhaps most followed his philosophy. Indeed, for the Zoramites, Korihor's approach was not just a philosophy but a religion. "They had a place built up in the center of their synagogue," we are told by Alma in the very next chapter, "a place for standing, which was high above the head."[51] One by one these Zoramites ascended this stand or "Rameumptom"[52] and repeated the same vainglorious prayer, a prayer in which they thanked God that they were better than other people. "Holy God," they prayed, "we believe that thou hast elected us to be thy holy children . . . and thou hast elected us that we shall be saved, whilst all around us are elected to be cast by thy wrath down to hell; for the which holiness, O God, we thank thee; and we also thank thee that thou hast elected us, that we may not be led away after the foolish traditions of our brethren, which doth bind them down to a belief of Christ, which doth lead their hearts to wander far from thee, our God. And again we thank thee, O God, that we are a chosen and a holy people. Amen."[53]

Clearly, these people felt very good about themselves. They

were positive and confident. They believed that they were favored of God. They were "up." And yet, in reading the story, the Lord makes it unmistakably clear that this way of feeling good about oneself is not at all a good thing, and that this way of feeling up is actually a spiritual downer.

Now, if we're not careful, we can easily begin to look down at the Zoramites from our own Rameumptoms. I know that I, for one, have at times ascended my own personal towers. For example, looking back, I can see how I sometimes turned something my parents taught me into a kind of Zoramite creed. "You're a Ferrell," my father would say to me, when speaking about the way one should live. "That means something. It means you *don't* do things like this and that, and that you *do* do things like that and this." He would look at me sternly and then ask, "Do you understand?" I would nod and then, as children sometimes do, find somewhere to go or something to do to escape from the teaching.

I think that I sometimes internalized a lesson from these experiences that my father wasn't teaching. Instead of learning about better and worse ways to behave, in some ways I learned, instead, to think that it was better to be a Ferrell than it was to be a Schmidt or a Dixon or a Cabrera. (I'm trying here not to name any people that I actually knew!) I had built a little Rameumptom of my own.

As I've grown older, I like to think that that bit of up-ness has fallen away, but what if I find that I am struggling with someone in my personal life and am upset that he or she is always so unreasonable! And what if I find myself complaining to and about them and praying to God that they will change (because, obviously, I'm not the one who needs to)? At that rate, it won't take long to build the tower anew.

The Rameumptom approach to happiness is so antithetical to the truth that the scriptures tell us not only that Alma was "astonished" by it when he witnessed it in the Zoramites, but that he was astonished "beyond all measure."[54] "Behold, O God," Alma cried in anguished faith, "they cry unto thee, and yet their hearts are swallowed up in their pride. Behold, O God, they cry unto thee with their mouths, while they are puffed up, even to greatness."[55] *Up is not up,* Alma is teaching us through his reaction and prayer. Happiness cannot be found by learning to glory in oneself. "Whosoever shall seek to save his life" in such a way, the Savior taught, "shall lose it."[56] So it turns out that Korihor's up doctrine is ultimately a downer. Happiness comes in a different way altogether.

Which begs the question: How? What if I'm feeling stuck in a really bad situation? What if I'm feeling worthless or overlooked or condemned? In these and other cases in which I might be feeling down, I might relate to another group of Zoramites—those who were themselves overlooked and made to feel worthless. It is to this humiliated group that Alma reveals the truth that completes the divine paradox.

5

THE FALSE BURDEN
OF DOWN

Alma and his brethren had been cast out of the Zoramites' synagogues because they were preaching against the doctrine of up. Another group was cast out as well—not because they disagreed with the doctrine, but because they found themselves on the losing end of it. These despised of the Zoramites were kept from their worship services because of "the coarseness of their apparel"[57] and their "exceeding poverty." "They have cast us out," they complained to Alma, "and we have no place to worship our God. . . . What shall we do?" they pleaded.[58]

Perhaps, like the poor Zoramites that Alma was speaking to, you have felt down. I certainly know what that feels like. On my first day in junior high school, for example, a young lady kicked me as I walked past her in the hall. I had never seen her before, and I had done nothing to provoke her (except, perhaps, breathe!). Already filled with anxiety in my new and intimidating surroundings, between classes I stayed nervously on the lookout for her. I wasn't vigilant enough, however, and she kicked me again the next day, this time hurling an insult while she did it. "Monkey ears!" she yelled. I felt as if everyone else in the hall was instantly looking at me, and I felt a withering embarrassment. I began looking at my reflection in windows and mirrors. I began seeing myself as she did.

A week or so into the school year, I noticed this same girl ahead of me on the street when I was walking home. From that day forward, I took a much longer route home. I also slowed my morning school preparations and began asking my mother to drive me to school. My blessed mother drove me to school every day for the rest of the year. I marvel and am so grateful that she never got after me for being so slow even though it put her out every morning. My shame had wired my mouth shut. How could I tell her or anyone else what was really going on? As a seventh-grade boy, and one who fancied himself an athletic kid who had things together, how could I confess to being so debilitatingly afraid? And of *a girl* at that!

Maybe, like the secret I carried as a seventh-grade boy, you have your own secrets that weigh you down. Or maybe you worry that other people don't like or accept you. Or perhaps you have other burdens. For example, maybe you have felt cracks in the foundation of your marriage. Or maybe your children have brought you heartache. Or perhaps you have been blessed with neither marriage nor children, and every family-related comment at church feels like a blow not only to your heart but also to the pillars of your faith. Maybe your professional life has been a personal disappointment. Perhaps your body is racked with pain and you look on in envy as others stroll effortlessly by you. Or perhaps your testimony is wavering, and you wonder if you have built your life upon a lie. Perhaps, like the poor Zoramites, you are wondering how to find the relief you are seeking.

Alma's first sentence to this group undoes much of what passes today as self-help wisdom. "I behold that ye are lowly in heart," he said, "and if so, blessed are ye."[59] In contrast to Korihor, Alma is saying that it is good that they are feeling down! And why is it a good thing? Alma answers that question this way:

> Because ye are compelled to be humble blessed are ye; for a [person] sometimes, if he is compelled to be humble, seeketh repentance; and now surely, whosoever repenteth shall find mercy.[60]

Notice what Alma is *not* saying. He is not saying that there is value in feeling down by itself. In fact, by itself, feeling down *is* a downer. There is a way of feeling bad (perhaps the most common way, in fact) that is just a way of feeling bad about

24

oneself. It is the way one feels bad when he or she is feeling down about not feeling up. It is a kind of depression or malaise or despair that we feel when we have bought in to the doctrine of up but believe we have failed under it. "We can distinguish more clearly," Elder Neal A. Maxwell taught, "between divine discontent and the devil's dissonance, between dissatisfaction with self and disdain for self. We need the first and must shun the second, remembering that when conscience calls to us . . . it is not solely to scold but also to beckon."[61] In his response to the poor Zoramites, Alma was speaking of the beckoning kind of lowliness Elder Maxwell describes. It is what feeling down feels like when one is down before the Lord rather than down on oneself.

When Alma told the poor of the Zoramites that it was a good thing that they were feeling lowly in heart, he was saying that feeling down gave them a chance to see what they had to see in order to be lifted: their sins, and therefore as well their need to repent. In response, these people might have been tempted to say: *Don't speak to us of further burdens. That just makes us feel worse! We are already down. If we now have to see our sinfulness, too, it will be more than we can bear!* To which Alma, had he been asked, might have said something like this: *It might seem that way to you, but it's a lie. It's what seeing one's faults looks like from the Christ-less perspective of the doctrine of up. It means failure. It means worthlessness. It means despair. But put down the chains of that doctrine and you will discover a truth you have never*

25

fully known. For the Lord's yoke truly is easy and his burden is light.[62] *In the moment you allow the Lord to show you your weakness, you will also experience his grace.*[63]

Think about it. When we brush up against God's presence, we are unavoidably reminded of how much we yet lack. This reminder of the chasm that exists between us and the Lord might seem like a depressing realization, but it is cause for despair only if we believe that we are left to cross that chasm ourselves. When we are down before the Lord rather than just down on ourselves, our understanding of the gulf between ourselves and God does not depress us. Why not? Because the Lord also warmly reassures us that our insufficiency in no way disqualifies us from his redeeming love. So rather than feeling despair, we put ourselves into a position where we can be filled with overwhelming gratitude and wonder—that God could love and redeem such a one as me! "Now, for this cause," Moses exclaimed without a hint of self-pity after an encounter with God, "I know that man is nothing, which thing I never had supposed."[64]

By thinking of the rich Zoramites, we see that *up* truly is *down*. This is because when we are feeling up in this way, we rely on what the scriptures call "the arm of flesh." In these moments, we aren't looking to the heavens as we must, which means that despite feeling personally strong or sufficient, we are truly down.

By pondering the situation of the poor Zoramites, however,

we realize that merely feeling down about oneself is no more helpful than feeling pridefully up about oneself. When we feel this way, we feel devoid of hope. And the reason we feel devoid of hope is because, perhaps without realizing it, in these moments we have bought into a philosophy that is devoid of Christ. In these moments, too, we are relying on the arm of flesh. We're just despairing because our own arms are so weak.

So while up is actually down, it turns out that down is also down unless we are down *before the Lord.* This is the lesson we learn from the group in Lehi's dream that fell down to partake of the fruit. They didn't merely fall down; they fell down *before the tree*—which is to say, they fell down before Christ. Only those who knelt humbly before him enjoyed the fruit of happiness. So to the paradox we have been discussing, we need to add a clarifying condition: Up is down and down is up, *so long as I am down before the Lord.* This is the divine paradox that brings peace to those who are feeling troubled, comfort to those whose hearts are broken, and hope to those who are on the brink of despair.

I don't want to be misunderstood on this point. I think there are many in the world who have experienced significant happiness in their lives even if they do not believe in Christ. Some of the best people I have ever known come from different religious traditions and belief structures, some of which do not include any concept of a Savior. But they love their families. They love their neighbors. They are honest and hardworking and humble. They are willing to see their faults and not to frantically ignore or gloss over them. They are humbly "down" as we have been discussing. And, when they are, I would suggest that they are humbly down before Christ even if they don't know that they are.

A passage in one of C. S. Lewis's books is instructive here. In the final book of the Chronicles of Narnia series, *The Last Battle,* there is an exchange between the Christ-figure, who is the lion Aslan, and a man who for all his life had been the devoted follower of a wicked and false god known as Tash. When he realized that he had been serving the wrong master, the man fell before Aslan, expecting to be destroyed. But Aslan—the "Glorious One"—"bent down his golden head and touched [the man's] forehead with his tongue" and said:

> Child, all the service thou hast done to Tash, I account as service done to me. . . . I take to me the services which thou hast done to him. For I and he are of such different kinds that no service which is vile can be done to me, and none which is not vile can be done to him. Therefore if any man swear by Tash and keep his oath for the oath's sake, it is by me that he has truly sworn, though he know it not, and it is I who reward him.[65]

I believe that the Lord's grace is immense enough that he blesses people with his Spirit even if they know nothing about it. The world over, there are those who are, in effect, kneeling before him even though they don't know who he is. But he knows who *they* are. He knows them, and he knows their hearts. And when they or we bow in humble recognition of our faults, we bow before him and are blessed of him.

As Alma began to teach the poor in spirit of the Zoramites, he knew, as Jesus would later declare, that "blessed are the poor in spirit *who come unto me,* for theirs is the kingdom of heaven."[66] In other words, being poor in spirit alone is not enough. As the divine paradox suggests, we must also come unto Christ. The poor of the Zoramites were feeling down. Alma's task was to help them feel down before the Lord, as their happiness depended upon their kneeling before the tree. So Alma proceeded to deliver to them one of the most well-known, yet perhaps least understood, sermons that we find in the Book of Mormon. Echoing Lehi's dream, it is the parable of a seed that grows into a tree—which tree bears fruit "which is most precious, which is sweet above all that is sweet, and which is white above all that is white, yea, and pure above all that is pure."[67]

The meekness that allows the Lord to lift our hearts and spirits begins, Alma taught, with faith. Not, however, with faith in general, but with faith of a particular and divine kind.

6

THE SEED OF HOPE

If we are feeling down and lacking hope, it turns out that we can't find the happiness or hope we are seeking by trying to increase either our happiness or our hope. Korihor would argue this point, of course, insisting that if we are feeling down, happiness is derived by lifting up our heads, glorying in our strengths, and asserting our rights and our privileges.[68] But the scriptures we have been considering suggest that it doesn't work that way. We don't ascend upward by trying to lift ourselves upward, a lesson as old as the Tower of Babel. The lifting of our souls is achieved indirectly, even paradoxically, as the result of a different quest—a quest not to find ourselves, but to find Him. Hope, and the happiness that comes with it, Mormon taught, is the natural and inevitable result of an increased faith in Christ.[69] This understanding was what Alma began to offer to the humbled Zoramites.

"Faith is not to have a perfect knowledge of things," Alma wrote. "Therefore if ye have faith ye hope for things which are not seen, which are true."[70] If all you can do is arouse yourself simply to have a desire to believe, he taught, then that will be enough to allow you to experiment upon the word of God and grow that humble openness first into faith and then into knowledge.[71] He famously likened this process to the planting and nourishing of a seed, which, if nourished correctly, "shall take root; and behold it shall be a tree springing up unto everlasting life."[72]

The thirty-second chapter of the book of Alma is often cited as the definitive explanation of faith. From the context, however, there is nothing to indicate that Alma was interested in or intending to speak about faith *in general.* He wasn't at all interested in developing faith in whether the sun will rise tomorrow, for example, or in helping the poor in spirit to develop faith in themselves. In fact, the latter message would have been antithetical to what he was trying to help them understand. After all, the prospect of a rising sun does not cause a swelling within one's breast, nor does it enlarge one's soul,[73] which is what Alma promised would follow the planting and nourishing of this seed. And the only thing that would swell or enlarge if one's faith in oneself increased would be one's head. No, Alma was not making a general statement about the principle of faith. He was speaking about a single and specific kind of faith—faith in the only unseen thing that can change one's soul the way he described.

As we discussed in the previous chapter, the problem facing the Zoramite poor was that they needed to fall in humility before Christ. But why would they feel the need or desire to do that if they didn't believe in him? These were people, after all, who were despairing that they were not being allowed to enter the synagogue, ascend the Rameumptom, and offer the same anti-Christ prayer as their brethren. Like Korihor, they regarded belief in Christ as foolishness that only shackled and bound down those who were unfortunate enough to possess it.[74] Alma was inviting them to test that assumption. Alma's experiment upon the word was actually an experiment upon the *Word*[75]—that is, an experiment as to the truth of the divinity of Christ. Plant *that* seed in your heart, he was telling them. Even if you can only *desire* to believe—that is, be open to believing—that will be enough to try the experiment and to prove Christ.[76] Humble yourselves enough to plant that desire in your downtrodden hearts, and then see what happens. That is what Alma was inviting.

Unfortunately, the first time through, Alma's audience missed the point of his message.[77] They had no conception yet that Alma was speaking of Christ. They were listening, and they were open. But they hadn't yet understood the point he was making. In response, Alma immediately began to correct this misunderstanding. He began quoting the writings of prophets who had testified of Jesus. He cited the prophet Zenos, who in his afflictions prayed heavenward, saying:

> Thou hast also heard me when I have been cast out and have been despised by mine enemies; yea, thou didst hear my cries. . . . And thou didst hear me because of mine afflictions and my sincerity; and it is because of thy Son that thou hast been thus merciful unto me, therefore I will cry unto thee in all mine afflictions, for in thee is my joy; for thou hast turned thy judgments away from me, because of thy Son.[78]

Can you hear how Alma selected this teaching about Christ precisely because it spoke so directly to the poor Zoramites? They, like Zenos, were troubled because they had been cast out and were despised. Unlike Zenos, however, they hadn't yet discovered the only antidote for the resulting burden they were carrying. They wanted the blessing of judgments being turned away from them, and Zenos's words pointed them to the answer: It is only through Christ that judgment is turned away, including the burden of self-judgment.

Underscoring this point, Alma quoted from the writings of the prophet Zenock: "Thou art angry, O Lord, with this people, because they will not understand thy mercies which thou hast bestowed upon them because of thy Son."[79] It was at this point in his teaching that Alma explicitly revealed the identity of the seed he was calling upon them to plant in their hearts:

Cast about your eyes and begin to believe in the Son of God, that he will come to redeem his people, and that he shall suffer and die to atone for their sins. . . . And now, my brethren, I desire that ye shall plant this word in your hearts, and as it beginneth to swell even so nourish it by your faith. And behold, it will become a tree, springing up in you unto everlasting life. And then may God grant unto you that your burdens may be light, through the joy of his Son.[80]

Plant *this* word in your hearts—the word of the divinity of Christ—then will your burdens be made light through his joy. This was Alma's message both to us and to those who were down. *Would you not now humble yourselves and begin to test whether or not this Christ can lift you?* Alma is asking. There is nothing so down that He can't lift it. As the tree of his divine reassurance and testimony grows within us, the promise is that it will lift our burdens and soothe our souls.

So if I am feeling down, the answer is to seek for an increase in my faith in the One who "descended below all things."[81] If I feel that I have been treated unfairly, the answer is the same—increased faith in him who suffered all of the unjust mistreatments of man.[82] If my whole world is crumbling around me, only faith in the One who can resurrect and restore all things will bring peace to my troubled soul. If we are down but do not yet feel lifted with hope, then we perhaps are not yet down enough before Christ. Perhaps we are down because we feel bad that we are not as up as other people seem to be. Or maybe we are depressed, as a friend recently told me she was feeling, because we feel that the enormity and weight of our own imperfection is too much for even the Lord to lift.

To the degree we are struggling to find ourselves, to find hope, and to find happiness, we would do well to experiment upon the Word, as Alma taught, and see whether the discouragement or despair we are feeling is not displaced by the swell of the Lord's love. How can we do this? The way Alma taught us—by learning all the words about Christ that we can learn, and by planting and nourishing each of them, individually, within our hearts. All that is good and true will produce the growth, and light, and life that Alma promised. As Lehi and Nephi taught, it is the fruit of that tree that has the capacity "to make one happy" and to fill our souls with "exceedingly great joy."[83]

Years ago, when I was a young man, I finally worked up the courage to go and speak to my bishop about something I had done. I didn't know whether it was something I needed to speak with him about, but as I read the scriptures and listened to talks and lessons at church, it weighed on me more and more. The longer I went without speaking to him, the heavier I felt. And the heavier I felt, the worse I thought of myself.

How can you reveal to one you love and admire something that might hurt that person's opinion of you? That wedge of self-worry—the desire to impress that is the offspring of the doctrine of up-ness—kept me mired in despair. Like the self-pitying poor of the Zoramites, having accepted the doctrine of up-ness, I had set myself up to wallow in the self-pity of down-ness.

I don't remember how it happened, but somehow, some way, that younger version of me eventually went to see his bishop. And that good, loving man, Bishop Nolan Brown, heard what I had to say and loved me none the less for it. That meeting was my first real lesson in the lifting, redeeming power of the Lord Jesus Christ. To this day, more than thirty years later, I still remember my walk home as the lightest, most freedom-filled moment of my life. The Lord had lifted my burden to such an extent that it literally felt like I was floating. His yoke *was* easy and his burden *was* light, just as he had promised. Even with all the wonderful things I have been blessed to experience since, I don't know if I have ever felt closer to heaven than I did that afternoon as a fifteen-year-old boy.

When I was burdened by my unconfessed worry, I certainly would not have described myself as happy. Given the choice, I probably would have wished that I could have avoided those down moments altogether. But had I been relieved of feeling them, I never would have discovered the unspeakable joy and happiness made possible through Christ. If others had tried to relieve me of the guilt I was feeling as a teenager, they might have thought they were doing me a favor. But the relief would have been to my condemnation. It would have kept me from falling down before the Lord and enjoying the fruit that is "desirable above all other fruit"—the fruit that fills with joy and makes one happy.[84]

Truly, what a blessing it is to be lowly in heart—for, just as Alma promised, when we seek to repent, we *shall* find mercy.[85] But what of the times that I am *not* compelled to be humble? What about the parts of me that continue to "look up with boldness"? If these blessings begin with a fall before Christ, what will awaken me from my slumber of pride and help me to see what I am not yet seeing?

My hope in this case lies in a sentence—not as in a string of words, but as in a declaration of guilt. In mortality, freedom depends on a finding of innocence. Guilt seems a negative and bad thing, something to be avoided at all costs. But this is exactly wrong with respect to eternity. Regarding spiritual matters, our prospects actually depend on the degree to which we are willing to recognize and admit our guilt! This means that anything that awakens us to our guilt is actually a most cherished and divine gift.

PART TWO

THE GIFT OF GUILT

7

GUILT AS MERCY

Think of two people: one who keeps all but one of the commandments, and another who keeps only one. I have sometimes posed this situation to people and then asked the following question: Which of these people is better—in other words, closer to God, to heaven, to salvation?

An interesting discussion normally follows. People want to know which commandment the first person failed to keep, for example, and which single commandment the second person kept. And they ask whether the second person even knew about the commandments he or she was failing to keep; for surely one wouldn't be responsible for things one didn't know, they reason. And so on.

These are interesting factors to consider. But I find it even more interesting that Jesus tries to free us from any concern about these issues. Think about some of his parables. The laborer in the vineyard who came at the end of the day received the same compensation as those who had worked from the beginning.[86] (Who was "better" in that case?) The "sinful" son was admitted into his father's house, while the apparently righteous one kept himself from entering.[87] (Who was the better one then?) The reviled Samaritan was positioned as the one to emulate, while the pious believers were used as examples of sin.[88] On another occasion, when the disciples were disputing among themselves who should be the greatest, Jesus corrected their impulse to compare themselves one to another by saying, "If any man desire to be first, the same shall be last of all."[89]

So what does this mean regarding the question of which of these people is best? I believe it means that there is something deeply wrong with the question. The clearest statement I know that gets to the heart of what is wrong with the question is in the book of James, the second chapter and tenth verse. It is perhaps the most astonishing verse in all the scriptures. Here is what James writes:

> For whosoever shall keep the whole law, and yet offend in one point, he is guilty of all.[90]

The verse takes my breath away. You might read it again just to take in what he is saying. What he says can't be right, can it? It can't be the case that a person who keeps the *whole* and *entire* law save one point is nevertheless by that single transgression just as guilty as the person who keeps *none* of the law! That can't be right, can it?

Two analogies might help us to understand James's point. Here is the first: We are like passengers in individual lifeboats, all of which have holes in them of our own making. The holes in some of the boats are larger than those in others, and some boats have more holes and others fewer. But no matter the size or number of the holes in our boats, the terrible truth is that each of us is sinking.

If these holes represent our sins, then we can also say that no matter the size or number of our sins, each of us is separated from God. This is not to say that all sins are of the same magnitude. It is to say, however, that all sins, of whatever magnitude, will keep us from God. (After all, it took only one transgression for Adam and Eve to be cast out of the Lord's presence.) This means that each of us needs the Savior as much as anyone else does. Whether one transgression or ninety and nine, our predicament is the same. This, I believe, is what James was referring to when he said that transgressors of the law of any and every stripe are, in effect, guilty of *all,* for even as the result of one transgression we suffer the full effect of the law, which is separation from God. Paul taught this same truth: "What things soever the law saith, it saith . . . [so that] all the world may become guilty before God."[91] Notice how

Paul says "*all* the world"—the keeper of the ninety and nine as well as the keeper of the one.

On the surface, this may seem like a harsh doctrine. However, I have come to believe it to be one of the most merciful aspects of the gospel. Why is being, in effect, "guilty of all" a merciful truth? Because it rescues us from two debilitating temptations. First, it exposes the folly of thinking ourselves better than others. If we are all sinking from holes of our own making, is there really any solace to be found in the idea that I am sinking more slowly than my neighbor? The gospel, Paul taught, removes all reasons for boasting.[92] And this is by divine and merciful design. How much would our patience and love one for another increase, for example, if each of us could remember the simple, merciful truth that no matter what others may have done or failed to do, we are just as separated from God as they are. Wouldn't this invite us to be more welcoming of others, less judgmental, and more forgiving? Wouldn't it forever expose the absurdity of the pride that says we are better, and instead invite us to appreciate and love one another? Wouldn't it keep our minds on the only thing that really matters—our own equal and complete need for a Savior?

There is another temptation that is rendered powerless by this truth. It is the temptation to get down and depressed at the thought that we are worse than others. Whatever I may have done or failed to do, I am no more separated from God than anyone else. Perhaps I have kept only one law while my neighbor has kept ninety and nine. The gulf that remains between each of us and God is nevertheless infinite. I need to do exactly what my neighbor needs to do: repentantly fall down before the Lord and rely on his merits to save.[93] What each of us must specifically do while spiritually kneeling before him may vary. If the holes in my boat are larger than those in another's, for example, there may be more people to whom I need to reach out. It may mean that the Lord will need to apply more material to the wounds in my hull. And that process may hurt. But there is no wound that he cannot heal, no gap that he cannot cover, no weakness that he cannot make strong, and no hole that doesn't need his infinite Atonement. If I had to be forgiven of more, the Lord says that I will ultimately love him all the more.[94] So the question that matters is not how large are the holes in my boat, or how many, but whether I am willing to acknowledge and allow the Lord to fix them.

Another analogy might help to complete the picture, this one a very interesting truth about light. It turns out that no matter our speed relative to light, light always moves toward or away from us at the same constant speed of 186,282 miles per second (the "speed of light"). Aside from the insane rate of speed, this may not sound like a big deal, but if we put it in simpler terms, this truth about light becomes quite bizarre—and illuminating as to James's message. To see just how bizarre and illuminating, let's think about what normal experience teaches us.

When I was growing up, my grandparents lived on a ranch about ninety minutes from my home. Most Saturdays, my father and I would drive to the ranch to move sprinkler pipe, fix fences, and help tend to the horses. The large, timbered entrance to the ranch stood at the end of a half-mile-long dirt road that paralleled Interstate 90 in eastern Washington. I used to stand at the freeway fence begging truckers to honk their horns by raising my arm and tugging down on an imaginary rope. To my delight, most of them obliged. Those trucks barreled past me at about seventy miles per hour, their horns blaring. I loved it. I used to do the same thing when I rode in cars next to those trucks. If we were doing sixty-nine miles per hour and the trucks were doing seventy, they would honk as they inched past us.

That's all well and good, you might be thinking, but what does this have to do with light? Well, if instead of watching trucks along I-90, I was actually watching beams of light go by, my experience would have been very different. I might not have noticed the difference while I stood along the highway, as the beams of light would have passed by me at their full speed, just like the trucks did (although incredibly faster!). But I would have noticed a most curious thing had I tried to catch one of those beams of light. Let's just imagine that my father's car, with some otherworldly modifications, could manage a top speed of one mile per hour less than the speed of light. In that case, you might expect that the beam of light in the next lane would slowly reach and inch past us, just like the trucks, its relative speed being merely one mile per hour more than ours. But that would not have been our experience. Instead, the beam of light would have roared past us as if we were standing still even though our speed was just one mile per hour less than the light's!

As crazy as it sounds, according to the work of Albert Einstein, which has been verified by physicists over the last century, no matter how fast we ourselves may be moving, light will always pass us at the full speed of light. Period. No matter what. Nothing else that we know of acts that way—only the otherworldly gift that we call light. There is nothing we can do to catch up to light, or even to gain on it. If James had written a verse about light, he might have said something like this: "For whosoever shall travel at nearly the speed of light, and yet go just one mile per hour slower, he shall still be passed by light at the entire speed of light."

This perplexing, mind-bending paradox regarding light is similar to what James is teaching us about our own state relative to the law and God. Our guilt under the law, he is saying, like the speed of light, is a constant. Keeping the commandments, although critical for reasons we will discuss, does not catch us up to God (whose glory is comprised of "light and truth"[95]). And a person who keeps more of the law than another is nevertheless outstripped infinitely by the glory of God.

When we see what James was trying to teach us—that we

are each of us equally, completely, and infinitely in need of the Lord—we recognize guilt for what it truly is: a gift. *Don't be diverted by the sins or "successes" of others,* James is warning us. *Your personal need for the Savior is not affected in the least by what others have or have not done. You are no better than your spouse, for example, no matter the evidence you think you are marshalling. And your membership in the Church doesn't make you better than others either. You need the Savior in exactly the same degree as your spouse and your neighbor and the nonmember detractor do—which is to say, infinitely. If you get caught up in thinking yourself better or worse than your brothers or sisters, you will have bought into the damnation of the doctrine of up-ness. Hear what I am saying. Realize that the justice of God, alone, leaves no one but God standing. And that is by design, for only those who have fallen before him can be lifted—lifted and made into beings that are far beyond not only our capacity but also our imagination.*

James states the truth about us so plainly and starkly that we are forced to see that there is no way that we, of ourselves, can escape the jaws of justice. The verse exposes our powerlessness. After all, who can overcome the burden of being guilty of all? The answer: only One.

James, the brother of that One, was trying to help us not to miss the truth about ourselves and about Him. It is a truth we will never really see—unless we begin to see the big picture.

8

THE BIG PICTURE

Why do we need to turn to Christ? And how, exactly, does the gospel invite us to turn to him?

To address these questions, we need to understand both our current condition and our eternal possibilities. What is our current condition? As we discussed in the last chapter, our condition is that we are separated from God. To use a metaphor from the last chapter, he is Light and we are not, and we are therefore inescapably apart from him. But what does this really mean?

Here, another analogy might help us. A good friend of mine spent many years as a judge. He presided over hundreds of drug cases. All were more or less just cases to him until, one day, he lifted his head to see his neighbor standing before him. Things were suddenly entirely more personal. And yet, there was a law, and that law had been broken. He might have liked to set his neighbor free, but what kind of justice would that be if he didn't do the same for all the others? But if he did the same for all the others as well, what would become of the notion of justice? Or mercy, for that matter? If none are guilty, then mercy is rendered meaningless as well.

So what problem confronted this neighbor? Two, actually. The first was that he had violated the law in a serious way, and these violations required punishment. In this case, the facts were such that the man needed to go to jail. And his friend was the one who needed to send him there. There is no escape from such personal consequence for violations of the laws of this world. The only way that a violator of such a law can be justified and set free again is for him to pay whatever consequence is associated with the transgression.

But this man had a second problem, even graver than the first. My friend has told me of the dismal repeat-offender statistics for drug users. After jail terms have been served, justifying their release, the overwhelming majority of offenders nationwide end up before yet another judge for the same or worse offenses and suffer the same consequence as before—over and over and over again. The first problem in such cases is that there has been a violation of the law, but the bigger problem is that the weaknesses and desires that led to those violations in the first place have not been overcome. Although their time served in prison had *justified* them in the eyes of the law for past offenses, it failed to *sanctify* them from the weaknesses and desires that had led them to commit those offenses and that would yet induce them to transgress in the future.

These twin principles of justification and sanctification play a central role in our own situations relative to God.[96] We, too, have two problems. The first is that we have violated the laws of God—our hands, the scriptures say, are "unclean." The second problem is that our hearts are impure—that is, we still desire things that are not holy.[97] Why is this a problem? Because anything that is unholy cannot be with God. We "must needs be sanctified from all unrighteousness," the scriptures say, "that [we] may be prepared for [his] glory."[98] "For he who is not able to abide the law of a celestial kingdom *cannot abide* a celestial glory."[99] In other words, unless and until our hearts and desires and wills are sanctified as the Lord's, we will never be able to be with and see the Father as he really is, in the fulness of his glory.[100] Which is to say that the only way to overcome the problem of never being able to catch up to light is to be made light ourselves.

The problem of life—the problem that the whole plan of salvation and redemption was conceived to solve—is how to transform and sanctify beings whose impure hearts, desires, and wills cannot abide the glory of God into beings whose hearts, desires, and wills *can* abide that glory. We are, as it were, the repeat drug offender. We must not only be justified or forgiven for past sins but must also be sanctified from *any desire* for sin.[101] How else could God entrust us with his power?[102]

God, like my friend the judge, might wish that he could waive the law in the case of those whom he loves, but to do so would frustrate the whole plan of happiness. Why? Because to waive the consequences of law would be to render law meaningless. *What's wrong with that?* one might respond, hopefully. *If we got rid of law, wouldn't we get rid of our problems? And wouldn't that make life so much easier and more enjoyable?* To which I would answer: "No, the law is a gift to us. Getting rid of it would mean that you and I would be doomed to an eternal hell."

Why is that?

Think about it. Even if God *could* waive the law without frustrating the plan of happiness, that would solve only the first of our problems—the problem of needing to be justified or forgiven of our sins. Waiving the law would not sanctify our hearts, and we therefore would still be separated from God. It turns out that laws or commandments are necessary in order for us to become sanctified. Here's why: We can overcome the desire for sinfulness only by being allowed to choose sinfulness. Where there is no choice to sin, there also can be no choice not to, and therefore no opportunity to overcome the desire for it. It was the establishment of the law that "created" the possibility of sin in the first place, for without the presence of the "right," there would be nothing that could be considered "wrong." "If . . . there is no law," Lehi taught, "there is no sin. [And if] there is no sin, [then there can be] no righteousness."[103]

Redemption is the process of sanctification through which the Lord, by his Spirit, refines and purifies our souls so that we "have no more disposition to do evil, but to do good continually."[104] "There is no flesh that can dwell in the presence of God," Lehi taught, "save it be through the merits, and mercy, and grace of the Holy Messiah."[105] The Savior took *our* impurities and proclivities toward sin upon himself and overcame them. His condescensions[106] below us all have given him the ability and power to change the hearts and dispositions of all who demonstrate that they want their hearts and dispositions to be changed. However, since it is our wills, themselves, that need to be changed, he cannot, without frustrating the whole plan of redemption, change us against our wills. He will change and lift only what we ask to be changed and lifted.

If, recognizing our broken sinfulness, we humbly and repentantly fall before him, begging in faith for his merciful forgiveness and healing, the Savior of the World, or "my Jesus," as Nephi intimately referred to him,[107] will fulfill his oath and his promise to heal and make us holy.[108] His work on our behalf is at once infinite and infinitesimal: It is so big that he offers redemption to all, and yet so small that he offers redemption to *me*—offering to cleanse and sanctify every particle of my soul, refining it through the fire of the Holy Ghost.

It follows from this that we need to see every piece of

ourselves that needs refining—every weakness, every fault, every failing, every transgression—so that we can offer it as a sacrifice to the Lord with a broken heart and contrite spirit. This is why attempts to pump ourselves up and think artificially well of ourselves can be so damaging. Happiness *depends* on us seeing our faults. The gospel "causes men and women to reveal that which would have slept in their dispositions until they dropped into their graves," Brigham Young taught. "The plan by which the Lord leads his people makes them reveal their thoughts and intents, and brings out every trait of disposition lurking in their [beings]. . . . Every fault that a person has will be made manifest, that it may be corrected by the Gospel of salvation."[109]

To the Zoramitish modern world, a world that is obsessed with people's looking and feeling good about themselves, this may sound like a depressing prescription. Can't you just hear Korihor saying, *Why do ye yoke yourselves down with such foolish things? Don't bind yourselves down. You're just fine—better than fine, actually. You're wonderful! Lift up your heads. You can do anything you set out to do. Look up with boldness![110]* But his words would be leading us astray and robbing us of the very happiness that he proclaims to be enabling. We are lifted "grace for grace,"[111] one disposition at a time. As we offer our weaknesses as sacrifices to the Lord, he will remove our sinfulness from us. But we need to see our weaknesses in order to offer them to him. Which begs this question: How, in this fallen world, will we be able to see what we need to see?

As we will discuss in the next chapter, the Lord reveals these truths to us through the mechanism of his commandments.

9

STUNG BY THE TRUTH

I offered one of our children an incentive (some might call it a bribe) to speed up his potty training. The deal was that if he could successfully go for a certain agreed period of time—I think it was a week or so, day and night—without using diapers or Pull-Ups, he could begin to ride the shiny new training-wheeled bike I had for him in the garage. He successfully completed his part of that deal on a Sunday morning. He had done his part, and I felt I therefore owed him mine, whatever the day or time. So, before church began, I agreed that I would walk beside him as he rode that little bike around the block, a distance of about one mile.

Halfway around, he tired of riding and asked me to pull the bike home for him. A bit perturbed, I bent down, grabbed the handlebars with my left hand, and began towing the bike. About ten steps later, my lower back began to spasm. It felt like my back muscles were attached to a dial that someone was turning. The pain doubled me over. Within seconds I couldn't even move. I remained on my feet, albeit bent over, only because I had the bike to lean on. I gasped for breath, wondering what I should do. After a minute or so, I found that I could slowly make my way home if I used the little bike as a walker.

When I got home, I quickly called someone to see if he could cover a class I was to teach. *There is no way I can go to church in this condition,* I thought. (My decision was made all the easier because I hadn't yet prepared a lesson!) I then grabbed a book I had been reading and carefully climbed down onto the floor and gingerly turned to my back. My Sabbath would be reading this gospel-related book, I told myself. I happened to open the book to the first page of a new chapter. I stared in surprise at the chapter title: "GO ANYWAY," it told me. I have lived through many coincidences, but that chapter title at that moment did not seem to be one of them. I was to be at church.

Commandments are a little bit like that chapter title. They are given to us to awaken us to something—to both a problem and a need. And the commandments I am finding the hardest to keep at any particular moment are the ones that are calling me out of my deeper slumbers. A little-known application of a well-known experience during Israel's wanderings in the wilderness will help us to understand this more clearly.

On an occasion in the wilderness when the Israelites started complaining against Moses because of the difficulty of the way, "the Lord sent fiery serpents among the people, and they bit the people; and much people of Israel died."[112] The people then came to Moses in the spirit of repentance and begged him to intercede for them before the Lord.[113] Moses did so, and the Lord instructed him to make a serpent out of brass and to set it on a pole. He was then instructed to command Israel to look upon the serpent of brass. All those who looked upon it lived.[114]

The scriptures confirm what one suspects when reading this story—that the brass serpent was a similitude of the Savior. "As Moses lifted up the serpent in the wilderness," John wrote, "even so must the Son of man be lifted up: That whosoever believeth in him should not perish, but have eternal life."[115] Here is a question that illuminates the role of the gospel, and specifically the commandments, in our lives: If the brass serpent is a type of the Savior, of what might the fiery serpents be a type? Consider this possibility: that the fiery serpents are a similitude of the commandments.

The law of Moses was largely an outward law of what the scriptures call "carnal commandments."[116] Its various behavioral rules were many and specific—so much so that it was essentially impossible for anyone to keep all of them perfectly. Sacrificial offerings were required for each transgression under the law, continually pointing Israel to the need for atonement yet at the same time hinting at the insufficiency of the law itself to do that since, as Paul said, "it is not possible that the blood of bulls and of goats should take away sins,"[117] nor "purge" man's "conscience" (that is, his desire or will) from a disposition to sin.[118]

Like the fiery serpents, the law of Moses was given to Israel to turn them to Christ. The law, like each serpent, was designed to "bite" Israel by awakening them to their sins and requiring them to seek atonement for them. Just as salvation from the poison of the fiery serpents required Israel to look to the representation of Christ that Moses raised on the pole, so salvation from transgressions under the law required them to look to the Lord himself.

Jesus announced that this outward law that was given unto Moses was "fulfilled" in Christ. "[It] hath an end in me,"[119] Jesus said. But he then commanded, "Look unto me, and endure to the end," and (this is important) "*keep my commandments.*"[120] He gave this same instruction to his apostles near the end of his mortal life: "If ye love me, *keep my commandments.*"[121] So his statement that the law of Moses—the law of outward performances—was fulfilled in him was not at all to say that the obligation to keep *commandments* was fulfilled in him. Far from it. He was just saying that the complicated set of outward laws that comprised the law of Moses—a set of laws with the sole purpose of pointing Israel to the coming of the Messiah—was fulfilled with the appearance of that Messiah.

While the commandments we are to live today may be less outwardly demanding than the law of Moses was, they are far more inwardly demanding. For example, it is not enough merely not to kill. The Lord now has commanded us not to be angry! Anyone who gets angry at another, he says, "shall be in danger of hell fire."[122] Likewise, we are not to lust, and we have been commanded not to let any such thoughts *"enter into [our] heart."*[123] The Savior also said that we are to be "meek,"[124] "merciful,"[125] and "pure in heart,"[126] with "bowels . . . full of charity towards all men."[127] It is not enough any longer merely to love one another; we are to love each other as Jesus has loved us.[128] And so on. No matter the excuses we feel we might have, it is like we are each staring at a page meant just for us that says, in effect, "Go Anyway"—*Love Anyway, Forgive Anyway, Be Grateful Anyway, Have Faith Anyway, Be Charitable Anyway.* If the ancient Israelites were bound to stumble by the strictness of their outward law, we are even more certain to stumble by the strictness of this inward law.

Our struggles to keep these deeper inward laws expose our need for the Savior just as transgressions of the law of Moses did. However, these deeper laws do something more than this. These are the laws of the celestial kingdom that we must be able to abide in order to abide the glory of that kingdom.[129] So when we break these laws, our unholiness itself is being exposed. The laws therefore not only cause us to turn to Christ for a forgiveness of sins (in order to justify us pertaining to the law), they also expose within us the weaknesses that we need him to change in us if we are to become as he is—not only without spot, but *holy*.[130] With this understanding, when we turn to Jesus, we fall before him not only for forgiveness but for the purging, purification, and *sanctification* of our souls.

Lehi's dream is instructive here. Of two absolutes in the dream, the first was that every person who failed to cling to the rod failed to make it to the tree. So it turns out that walking in the vicinity of the commandments is not enough. For protection's sake, we must *cling* to that rod—like Helaman's stripling warriors, we must "observe to perform every word of command *with exactness*."[131] To which you might object: *But we DON'T perform every word with exactness! And because we don't, we are therefore, each of us, separated from God and, in effect, "guilty of all."* And you would be exactly right.

However, here is the crucial point: Being guilty of all does *not* mean that we are no longer clinging to the rod! On the contrary, it is precisely *because* we are clinging to the rod that we recognize in the first place that we are guilty. The word of God is what gives us the standard. It is precisely because we have committed to live to that standard with exactness that we are awakened to our sins—that is, to our failure to live that standard with exactness. So the rod—the law—is what establishes our guilt. And the tightest-gripped, most exactingly obedient moments we ever display are when we are repenting of our failures under the law, as repentance is itself the central provision or

61

commandment of the rod of iron: "Now this is the command-ment," Jesus announced, "Repent, all ye ends of the earth, and come unto me . . . that ye may be sanctified by the reception of the Holy Ghost, that ye may stand spotless before me at the last day."[132] "I have given you the law and the commandments of my Father, [so] that ye shall repent of your sins, and come unto me with a broken heart and a contrite spirit."[133] "Whosover [repenteth and] cometh unto me with a broken heart and a con-trite spirit, . . . him will I receive, for of such is the kingdom of God."[134]

Think about it. The kingdom of God is comprised not of the impressive and the beautiful but of the broken and guilty who come unto Christ. This brings us to the second absolute in Lehi's dream: Every person who fell down to partake of the fruit stayed at the tree. Guilt, being the only thing that turns us sufficiently to the Lord, truly is a gift—one of the greatest of all the gifts of God.

10

PRIDE IN DISGUISE

As we discussed in the previous chapter, the commandments act as a kind of pride buster. They offer all of us who believe that "all is well in Zion"[135] the chance to discover and repent of our sins. However, sometimes we can struggle with another kind of pride—a pride that masquerades as humility. When we are burdened with this kind of up-ness, we notice every personal violation of a commandment and, rather than allow the knowledge of sin to bring us humbly and repentantly to Christ, our self-concern causes us to bury our heads in despair. In these moments, we feel worthless before the Lord—worthless because we are not doing all that the Lord has commanded. And so we don't allow our imperfections to bring us to Christ, but rather because of our imperfections turn away from him and into ourselves. This move looks like humility, but it is one of the subtlest varieties of pride available to us. I know, because I have been there.

Years ago, before the Church instituted the three-hour block schedule for our Sunday meetings, we used to go to the chapel for meetings three times every Sunday—once in the morning for priesthood meeting, a second time for Sunday School opening exercises and classes, and finally a third time for a ninety-minute sacrament meeting. When I was a very young man, our ward's Sunday School superintendent, Brother Marchant, came to our class one Sunday to ask for volunteers who would be willing to give the prayer, the 2½-minute talks, and the sacrament gem (a verse of scripture shared before the sacrament was passed) in the following week's Sunday School opening exercises. My strategy was to quickly volunteer to say either the prayer or the sacrament gem. I was motivated by the desire to avoid having to give a talk at all costs! Unfortunately for me, I wasn't the only person in the class with that strategy, and I missed out on my first choice, the prayer. I *was* quick enough, however, to score the sacrament gem assignment. Given the other alternative, I felt lucky.

That week I memorized my scripture, and I arrived early the following Sunday to sit on the stand. As the meeting got under way, however, I realized that I didn't know for sure at what point in the meeting I was to stand up and recite my scripture. I asked the young man who had been assigned the talk if he knew, but he was as unsure as I was. I began to search my memory in panic. My memories of all the Sundays I had witnessed immediately cured into a single mass of impenetrable concrete. I had no idea when my turn was.

So I guessed.

Unfortunately, I guessed wrong. I had made it through nearly all of my scripture when I felt Brother Marchant's huge hand on my shoulder. Stretching himself to his full height just to my left, he said to the congregation, "I'd like to thank Jimmy for his outstanding preparation and enthusiasm." Then he turned to me and whispered, "You don't go until after the talks."

I was mortified. I caught a glance of my mother as I turned to take my seat, and I could tell that she was embarrassed for me as well, which made me feel even lower.

I tried to calm myself when I sat back down. Although my cheeks and ears burned with embarrassment, I was slowly gathering my composure when a new thought sent me tumbling into panic once more. *Brother Marchant said I was to give my scripture after the talks, but he didn't say WHEN after them!* Now I was really worried. I tried to get Brother Marchant's attention without being too obvious, but he didn't notice me. I didn't know what to do.

So I guessed again.

Right after the last talk, I rose again and started to recite my scripture. I knew something was wrong when I glanced down at our organist, Sister Hubbert, whose pained look signaled that I would soon be feeling Brother Marchant's hand again.

This time he just tugged on my pocket. "I will nod at you when you are to go," he whispered. I staggered back to my seat like a drunkard. I'm not being literary here. I really did fake a drunkard's walk, which of course made me feel even more stupid when the ridiculousness of that act hit me. I made sure that I didn't glance over at my mother.

I am probably the only person in the history of the Church who has offered the sacrament gem three times in a single meeting. At that moment, and at my age, the thought crushed me. I ran from the building the moment the meeting ended. I exited from the side door of the chapel and escaped into the ignorant and nonjudgmental outdoors. I sprinted home. I wouldn't be going to class, and there was no way I was going back to sacrament meeting. In fact, I remember vowing that I would never go to church again.

Since I was so down in that moment, you might think that I darted from the church a humble soul. That wouldn't be the truth, however. Feeling humiliated is a world apart from feeling humble. Humiliation is what one feels when one's *pride* has been injured. Whenever we are feeling down about feeling down, we have become consumed with ourselves every bit as much as those who are feeling up about feeling up.

When we are burdened by feelings of inadequacy, we are

failing to understand two freeing truths. The first is that we are not yet grasping that, with respect to the law, every person is both equally separated from God and equally "rescuable" by him. Downtrodden pride doesn't believe that. When suffering from this kind of pride, we believe, instead, that we are guiltier or more broken than others—in some cases, even irretrievably so. We know that we've been commanded to love, for example, but we are keenly and painfully aware of how often our hearts are raging, even when we are outwardly doing good. And we feel terrible about this. We feel guilty, but we are not humble, despite appearances. We are mad at ourselves that we are not as good as we want to be—as we believe we need to be.

The second great truth we are missing is that we do not yet understand and have faith in the Lord's mission to redeem us. Although we might understand the point in our minds, our hearts do not yet believe that this redemption does not depend on our perfection. It is well that we are taking the Lord's commandments seriously, but we are at the same time taking ourselves too seriously and him not seriously enough. We are in the middle of a misunderstanding that Paul was trying to rectify in his readers when he explained that we are justified not by our deeds but by faith—that is, by Christ.[136]

When I have been burdened with this version of pride, I have observed in myself one of two outward styles. The first style is a kind of hyperactive righteousness—an exhausting obsession with doing outwardly good things that loves *itself* doing the good things more than it loves those good things or the people for whom they are done. When we are living this way, every moment is a moment to prove ourselves, and we are consumed with how others are regarding us. The story of Martha in the tenth chapter of Luke can be read as an example of this. She had received the Master into her house in Bethany. While her sister, Mary, "sat at Jesus' feet, and heard his word," the scripture says that "Martha was cumbered about much serving, and came to him, and said, Lord, dost thou not care that my sister hath left me to serve alone? bid her therefore that she help me. And Jesus answered and said unto her, Martha, Martha, thou art careful and troubled about many things: But one thing is needful: and Mary hath chosen that good part, which shall not be taken away from her."[137]

On occasion, I have heard this story interpreted in ways that are attempts to ennoble Martha and absolve her of any wrongdoing—perhaps as a way to preserve the feelings of any of us who have ever played the part of Martha in our own lives. (And who hasn't?) But I think we risk missing the point when we do this, and, in fact, can become "cumbered about" in our interpretations. It is okay to have a problem. It is okay for Martha to have a problem. It is okay for Mary to have a problem. The healer of those problems was sitting in their home. But on this occasion, Martha, just as I know I frequently am, was too cumbered about and troubled about many things—her *own* things, such as the sufficiency of her meal, perhaps the state of her house, and so on—to receive the peace that was sitting right before her. "But didn't people need to eat?" one might object in defense. To which I would only observe that Jesus didn't rebuke Martha for her work but for her feelings. At least on the surface, the story may well be an example of an outwardly frantic style of downtrodden up-ness—the need always to look good or to be recognized as thoughtful. It is a *personal* need, a need necessitated by pride. When we suffer from this kind of pride, we don't just serve but "are cumbered about much serving," and are "careful and troubled about many things."[138]

The second style, by contrast, is a kind of giving up and shutting down. It is what I was doing when I vowed never to go to church again. Jesus spoke of this in his parable of the talents.[139] You know the story. A man gathered his servants to him before he left on a long trip. He divided his property between them—to one servant five talents (a very large sum of money), to a second two talents, and to the third one talent. The servant who had received five talents used them to produce an additional five talents for a total of ten. The second servant did the same, doubling his two talents for a total of four. The third servant, however, thinking his lord a judgmental and "hard man,"[140] and perhaps feeling like he was not as favored as the other servants, was afraid and hid his lone talent in the earth.

Upon their lord's return, they were asked for an accounting. To the first two servants, who had doubled their property, the lord said, "Well done, thou good and faithful servant: thou hast been faithful over a few things, I will make thee ruler over many things: enter thou into the joy of thy lord."[141] However, upon hearing the report from the servant who had hid his talent, he said: "Thou wicked and slothful servant, thou . . . oughtest . . . to have put my money to the exchangers, and then at my coming I should have received mine own with [interest]. Take therefore the talent from him, and give it unto him which hath ten talents. For unto every one that hath shall be given, and he shall have abundance: but from him that hath not shall be taken away even that which he hath."[142]

This parable reveals, among other things, that any kind of self-concern, including a self-concern that leads one to shut down and give up (as, for example, a fear to fail) is itself a kind of pride. Feeling depressed that I am worse than others is as much an act of pride as feeling myself better. Both are acts of self-concern—with oneself, rather than Christ, at the center.

The gospel, by its very nature, is designed to strip us of pride—of either the "I am better" or "I am worse" variety. And what is to take its place? The simple realization that "I am in need of Him." The gospel is designed to rescue us from our concern for self by making us equally in need of the same merciful Other—One who loves us (and our neighbors) infinitely, no matter what we (and our neighbors) might have done.

11

THE REPENTANT PATH

During a long plane ride a few years ago, I learned a great lesson about how the Lord strips us of pride, and how the resulting guilt turns to our good. After finishing the work I needed to get done on the flight, I put my things away and began mindlessly surfing the menu on the seatback screen to see if there was anything worth watching. (Think about how completely the miraculous can become mundane. From a vantage point that anciently could have been occupied only by heavenly beings, my primary concern was what to watch on TV!)

Nothing in particular interested me, and for a moment I contemplated a nap. With the thought that perhaps a slow and lousy movie could help me to sleep, I selected a show that at least had an actor I admired. I leaned back to watch, yearning for leaden eyelids. What I received instead was a lightning bolt to the heart.

The movie itself was unremarkable. An elderly woman was dying, and the narrative took us back to scenes from her life. At that level, the story was like many I have seen. But for some reason, on this mechanical, aimless day, the perspective of a life lived compelled me to evaluate the life I was then living. From within the cocoon of the plane, I felt pressure building within me. Something was trying to burst out—some truth, some insight, some yearning—something I needed to know about myself. I felt it in the tears that tumbled down my cheeks as the movie by proxy invited me to see my life from my own dying eyes. The old, expiring version of myself knew with clarity something that the striving, effort-filled, middle-aged version of me was missing. That lesson was at the tip of my soul's tongue. I could feel it, almost taste it, even. I felt an overwhelming desire to write.

Hastily, I pulled some paper from my bag. I put the tray table down and set the paper on it. Inhaling deeply, I wiped the water from my eyes and began writing. This is what burst from my pen:

> You try all your life to be somebody—well thought of, accomplished, substantial—and then in a flash of light you realize: it was an ill quest. And unnecessary. The things of import are right before us—all around

us, even. Offering ourselves in love to those around us is the work of greatest import. Nay, work it is not; it is all there is. And to find joy in all there is is to have found Him who made himself of no import that we too might choose each other over fame, selflessness over admiration, oneness over glory. And when we do, the glory comes.

Life's irony: Lose yourself and you find; live to find, and you never really live.

Every word cut deeply yet gently, each thought at once devastating and hopeful.

As I fell back into my seat, I knew two things as clearly as I had ever known anything. First, I knew that the way I had been living my life was somehow fundamentally amiss. It wasn't that I had committed any grave outward sin. On the contrary, it was that the Spirit was compelling me to consider how my apparent outward gospel compliance had blinded me to a spiritual rot that was nevertheless eating away within. I was being chastised about what the Lord called "the weightier matters of the law"[143]—the matters of the heart, or what I have come to understand to be "the deeper gospel." "Ye . . . outwardly appear righteous unto men," he chastised the scribes and Pharisees, "but within ye are full of hypocrisy and iniquity."[144]

What I had written suggested that I had been specializing in living the gospel outwardly and had in some ways mistaken that effort for living it inwardly. "Thou blind Pharisee," I felt the Savior speaking to me, "cleanse first that which is within the cup and platter, that the outside of them may be clean also."[145] My own pen had revealed my guilt.

But this brings me to the second thing that I knew as I leaned back in my seat: My soul was on fire. The Spirit had filled my breast and made even my extremities tingle with warmth. I knew that God was mindful of me; the flame of his Spirit reassured me of his love. Being guilty before the Lord did not keep me from his love. On the contrary, it was the guilt that he helped me to see that invited me to him.

I have noticed in myself how I sometimes prefer to focus on the happy topic of receiving forgiveness rather than on what seems like this hard and difficult and discouraging work of repentance. But when I am feeling this way, I am in the middle of a misunderstanding. The repentant path is the path of happiness.[146] It is only to those who are on that path that the Lord can say, "Be of good comfort, for I . . . will . . . ease the burdens which are put upon your shoulders, that even you cannot feel them upon your backs."[147]

My misunderstanding in these moments goes even deeper than this. I do need to be forgiven for the sins I have committed—that is the work of justification. The greater work, however, remains: the work of sanctification. And that is achieved not through forgiveness but through repentance. Between the two, repentance is the even greater gift. Alma was making this point when he said, "May the Lord grant unto you repentance."[148] Notice he does not say, "May the Lord grant unto you forgiveness." I'll repeat it again: *"May the Lord grant unto you repentance."* Elder D. Todd Christofferson spoke of the gift that is repentance in his October 2011 general conference address.[149] Paul, too, oriented us to this gift when he said that what we need is for "God [to] peradventure . . . *give [us] repentance* to the acknowledging of the truth."[150]

Thinking of the ordinance of baptism, which is the gate by which we enter the path that leads to eternal life,[151] we most often associate it with forgiveness. However, there isn't a single verse in the scriptures that links the word *baptism* with the word *forgiveness*. Rather, the linkage is with the word *repentance.* We are baptized, the scriptures say, "unto repentance."[152] "I . . . baptize you with water unto repentance,"[153] John the Baptist declared. Another verse says of him, "John did . . . preach the baptism of repentance for the remission of sins."[154] The word *remission,* here, is often read to be synonymous with *forgiveness,* but I don't believe that is an accurate rendering. To be baptized is to begin clinging to a rod that is designed to put sinfulness into remission within us. *Remission* refers not only to forgiveness of past sins but also to sanctification from future ones.

As we cling to the word of God, we will continually be awakened to the additional repentance that is needed. Early on, the rod of iron teaches us of the outward laws we are to obey. Relatively speaking, these are the easier laws. We learn regarding tithing, for example, and the Word of Wisdom, that "clinging to the rod" means keeping those laws with exactness *no matter the external circumstances.* As we grow in the gospel, however, the rod and its path will take us to deeper and more difficult places—to the interior terrain of our hearts, where holiness is formed. The law commands us to love, for example, to be charitable, and not to judge, to be angry, or to be envious. And at that level of life we must learn anew the same lesson—that clinging to the rod means that we will live by these standards toward others *no matter the external circumstances*—no matter what, for example, another has or hasn't done to (or for) us. When we meet circumstances where we are struggling to do this, we have just entered our own personal mists of darkness. The temptation will be to let go of the demand of the law. But we must remember: *This is the path not of perfection but of repentance.* We remain on that path so long as our hearts are broken and our spirits contrite, believing in the Creator of the rod enough to allow his words to invite us, once again, to repent of our failings.

From the perspective of the gospel of up, it seems a hard and foolish thing. The multitudes in the great and spacious building certainly think so, pointing their fingers and mocking those who continue to press forward and struggle—especially since, from their point of view, the ease of life in the great building is so appealing and ever available.[155] But the ease of up-ness is an illusion. The pride of the world always fails to deliver, as its promises are mere vapor, untethered either to law or to reality.[156] "And the fall" of those who put trust in those promises is "exceedingly great."[157]

What the observers in the building don't understand is that those who are struggling along the path, clinging to the rod, are being supported in their struggles by the Lord. They are not merely walking, they are being *changed*—one repentant step at a time. As a young missionary in the city of Gifu, Japan, I remember watching in awesome wonder as Brother Ono, a member of the ward, passed the sacrament every Sunday cradling the tray as he would a babe, tears streaming down his cheeks. Upon seeing his tears, those in the great and spacious building would presume a burden that didn't exist. "Come and be relieved of whatever troubles you," they might call to him. But his tears were already in relief. He was crying for joy. The joy of the tree stretches back along the rod of iron, and the travelers become filled with what Nephi called a "perfect brightness of hope."[158] What seems a burden is a delight.

"This is the way," Nephi declared, "and there is none other"[159]—none other way to real happiness and lasting joy. The way to happiness is to let the rod deliver us in humility at the Lord's feet. "Let your laughter be turned to mourning," James taught, "and your joy to heaviness. Humble yourselves in the sight of the Lord, and he shall lift you up."[160]

Any counsel that invites me to reach up rather than fall down will ultimately keep me from the joy that awaits in the

Lord's embrace. Such counsel, although appealing to the carnal spirit, is an invitation to join the throngs in the building rather than the disciples on the path, who are anxiously engaged in the happy effort of repenting.

Unfortunately, I still see the building and some of its philosophies in myself—particularly when things get difficult. I would like to consider with you some of the "pleasing" things I sometimes feel myself thinking, or hear myself or others saying, that I believe are coming from across the terrible gulf rather than from the direction of the tree.

After all, one of the things that we must repent of is the desire to join the voices in the building.

PART THREE

SIGNS OF UP-NESS

12

RULES WITHOUT HEART

If the doctrine of up-ness is a barrier both to happiness and to exaltation, as I believe it is, it is important to root any allegiance we might have to it from our hearts. Beginning in this chapter and continuing through chapter 18, I would like to explore with you some of the signs of up-ness that can caress our egos and bind our souls. Most of these symptoms are things I recognize because I have suffered with them myself to one degree or another. I'd like to begin with a symptom of up-ness that sets us up for many of the others—a shallow kind of gospel focus that blinds us to our own sins and makes it more likely that we will stumble over the sins of others.

With our first child, I remember how I went overboard trying to get him to progress and learn quickly: I hung a basketball hoop in his crib, taped an image of a piano keyboard to the ceiling, and generally overwhelmed him with attention. I suppose I was kind of a father on steroids. During this phase, when our son was six or so, I remember driving with him while quizzing him on, of all things, multiplication! I know, pathetic.

Anyway, I asked him what three times four equaled.

"Eleven," he answered.

"No, Son," I moaned. "Come on, we've worked on this. It's not eleven. Multiplying is just a quick way to add. So 'three times four' is just like adding three fours together: four plus four is eight, plus another four equals twelve. Got it? Okay," I pressed, "let's try that again. What's three times four?" I looked at his reflection in the rearview mirror as we drove. "Come on, what is it?"

My little boy puffed out his chest and lifted his chin. "Eleven!" he shot back.

I certainly got what I deserved, but the story taught me a deeper point. Although I was right on the math, I was wrong about something else—what you might think of as a deeper kind of math—the spiritual arithmetic, if you will, that governs our relationships. And when we are wrong in this deeper way, it tends to ruin everything else.

When Jesus appeared to the Nephites, he expressed concern about a dispute they were having over the manner of baptism.[161] "There shall be no disputations among you, as there have hitherto been," he said, "neither shall there be disputations among you concerning points of my doctrine, as there have hitherto been. For verily, verily I say unto you, he that hath the spirit of contention is not of me."[162] Think about it: He chastised all parties to the argument even though, presumably, some probably had been *right*. Jesus was teaching that righteousness and discipleship are not simply a function of getting the gospel details right. He was teaching them, and us, that there is a deeper gospel, and that if we want to be his disciples, we must live the gospel in this deeper way. He makes a similar point in section 50 of the Doctrine and Covenants. There he declares that if we preach the truth without his Spirit, our teaching is not of God.[163] Think about it: This implies that if we don't have the Spirit, what we are saying is not of God even if what we are saying is true! Once again, there appears to be a deeper truth than what we say, or teach, or do, and we are not the Lord's disciples unless we are striving to live truthfully at this deeper level.

What is this deeper level? As we discussed earlier, the Lord requires that we live the gospel at the level where holiness is forged—*at the level of our hearts*.[164] "For behold," Mormon taught, "if [a man] offereth a gift, or prayeth unto God, except he shall do it with real intent it profiteth him nothing. For behold, it is not counted unto him for righteousness. . . . If a man . . . giveth a gift . . . grudgingly, . . . it is counted unto him the same as if he had retained the gift; wherefore he is counted evil before God. And likewise also is it counted evil unto a man, if he shall pray and not with real intent of heart; yea, and it profiteth him nothing, for God receiveth none such."[165]

This may seem to be an impossible standard, as our hearts so often are not pure. But when we look at Mormon's words, I think the standard is not as impossible as it may seem. Mormon says that if we give a gift grudgingly it is counted the same as if we hadn't given it at all. Don't our own lives tell us that this is so? When we drive our kids somewhere, for example, but do so angrily, are the kids likely to respond gratefully? If I do something my spouse wants me to do but do it resentfully, isn't my spouse likely to respond to me in about the same fashion she would have had I refused to do it at all? Mormon is making a statement here not merely about how our actions are received by the Lord but also about how they are received by our fellow beings. It turns out that children, spouses, siblings, neighbors, coworkers, parents, and the other people in our lives all respond to us based on what they *feel* from us. This is often why our otherwise helpful outward actions are sometimes dismissed by others, or unappreciated, or ignored. If they sense that our outward kindness is really just masking an inward resentment, they do not "count our actions for righteousness" but rather count them as if we hadn't done them at all.

So it seems it is with God, although for an entirely different reason. The Lord wishes to bless us and change us. He wants us to pray to him, for example, so that he can speak with us, but what can he do if we are just going through the motions? However, Mormon's words don't imply a standard of perfection at the level of our hearts but rather a standard of meekness and humility. Having real intent doesn't mean that I am perfect. It may mean that I really want to do what is right and to do it in the right spirit, even if I am presently struggling to do so. That would certainly be a soul that the Lord could bless. And while my intentions in giving a gift may not be perfect, I may offer a gift wishing that I could love more than I do and hoping that the Lord could help me. That would be a long way from doing something grudgingly. In fact, it would be the kind of humble offering that the Lord could make beautiful.

"When thou doest thine alms," the Lord taught, "do not sound a trumpet before thee, as the hypocrites do in the synagogues and in the streets, that they may have glory of men. . . . But when thou doest alms, let not thy left hand know what thy right hand doeth."[166] I don't know about you, but I find that last bit remarkable. What does it mean that one hand doesn't even know what the other is doing? I believe it means that when our hearts are yielded humbly to God, and our former self-concern is replaced with concern for others and for the Lord, we feel neither the need nor the desire to claim righteousness—whether to persuade our own minds or the minds of others on that subject. Because of this, we have no need to take note of, or relish in, any "good" that we do. Our left hands don't even notice what our right hands are doing. They don't need to. They aren't trying to prove anything.

The brilliant British writer G. K. Chesterton echoed this insight: "How much larger your life would be if your self could become smaller in it; if you could really look at other men [and women] with common curiosity and pleasure. . . . You would break out of this tiny and tawdry theatre in which your own little plot is always being played, and you would find yourself under a freer sky, and in a street full of splendid strangers."[167]

Part of the tininess of life when we are burdened by up-ness is due to the fact that up-ness is always focused on the shallow aspects of the gospel rather than upon the deep. At the level of my outward performances, I may be able to consider myself better than my neighbor, but a focus on the deeper gospel—on the state of my heart—never allows this. In the moment I believe myself purer than others, I become least pure. When I think myself more humble than others, my humility is gone. To see myself as the one who serves most is to reveal myself as one who has not been serving at all.

"[The outward laws] ought ye to [do]," Jesus reassured the Pharisees. But then he moved the earth from beneath their self-assured feet when he added that in addition they must "not leave the [inward laws] undone."[168] This is a passage that I had quite forgotten one day when I ran out of gas on a freeway.

13

UNACCEPTABLE
AND ACCEPTABLE SINS

A decade or so ago, needing to leave a family reunion a day early to get home for work, I hopped a ride with a cousin, her friend, and one of my brothers-in-law. I was significantly older than the rest and, theoretically at least, the most responsible.

Just fifteen miles from my home, the car began to cough and sputter, and then it quickly died. We coasted to the side of the freeway, out of gas. The next exit was a mile ahead. We were discussing who might go look for a gas station when a passing car slowed and pulled to the shoulder fifty yards in front of us. I remember looking at the car and thinking that it was in worse shape than ours. The rattling car backed up a bit and stopped. Then all four doors opened simultaneously.

Sometimes memory can play tricks on you. I remember returning to the home of my youth, for example, and finding it and the yard much smaller than I had remembered. The epic battles that we had waged in the backyard just couldn't have happened on that small plot of ground. But they had—perhaps a little less heroically than I had remembered. My memory of those climbing from the car in front of us may be of this sort—part what really happened mixed with what my mind has dreamed up over the years. In any case, here is what I remember: Four teenagers emerged from the car, each of them dressed in black. One of them had a green mohawk that stood eight inches tall. Another had a nose ring. All of them were accessorized with an ample number of chains.

They walked toward us, and I remember thinking, *We're going to DIE.* The four of us climbed out of our car to meet them. As they strode up to us, one of them asked, "You having some trouble?"

"It looks like we're out of gas," one of us responded.

To which one of them said, "We can take one of you for some gas."

Silence. The oldest of our group (me) looked down at his feet. *Someone might die today,* I thought to myself, *but it isn't going to be me.* As I still gazed at the ground, I heard my brother-in-law say, "I can come with you." A moment or two later I lifted my head to see him trudging off with the leather posse.

Fifteen minutes later, this group of teenagers dropped him

off at our car with a container full of gas. Wishing us well, they waved good-bye and continued on their way.

I have reflected on this experience many times over the years. Here was this group of young people doing for me what I, honestly, had never done for another. How many broken-down cars have I passed and not helped—even when safety would not have been a worry? Even worse, how many have I passed and not even noticed? And yet there I was passing judgment on those who were putting themselves out to help me.

And on what grounds?

I was looking down at a teenage boy because he had green hair, and at the others because of their love of chains. Somehow I felt that my clean-shaven face and closely cropped hair made me the better. But I was not "looking at the heart of man," as we are told the Lord does.[169] It might be true that I looked more like our modern-day prophets have taught us to look. But I somehow had drawn a conclusion from this that the same prophets had never themselves drawn—that such obedience justifies my thinking that I am better than others. The irony, of course, is that the disciples that day on the highway were dressed in black and sported chains. Who was closer to God—the man with the missionary haircut who was feeling superior or the teenager with the spiky hair who was loving his neighbor? That day, those young people worried me. Today, I pray to God that I can learn to have the kind of charity that they exhibited toward me.

I shared this story in a fireside a few years ago, talking about what I hoped I had learned from that and other experiences—about not to judge, for example, and about extending mercy to our fellow man. Afterward, a woman came up and thanked me for my remarks. She said that she hoped I could help her with something. I smiled and mumbled some kind of trite reply. And then she explained that she was worrying over an upcoming family reunion of her own. I could tell by her tone and facial expressions that she was really weighed down about something. "You see," she said, "my sister is a lesbian." She paused for a moment before continuing. "What do you think?" she asked earnestly. "Do you think we should allow her to come?" My heart broke at the question.

This good sister, like me that day on the highway, was suffering from what I sometimes call "the myth of socially acceptable and unacceptable sins." There seems to be a social pact of sorts—a collective judgment—that certain kinds of behaviors are so reprehensible or else so rebellious that we are released from the obligation to love those who struggle with them. In these moments, without realizing it, we have made socially acceptable our own breaking of the second great commandment. In our piety, we have ascended our own Rameumptoms and have cast others out of the synagogue.

A good friend, after being called as a stake president, placed ashtrays at the entrances of the buildings in his stake. "No one," he announced in stake conference, "should feel unwelcome at church because they smoke. After all, each of us is struggling with something, and *we* are still welcome here. Why should those who still struggle with smoking not be able to share the pews with those of us who are still struggling in other ways?" And with that, this good stake president invited the members of his stake to leave their personal Rameumptoms at home—or, better yet, to dismantle them altogether.

As I understand the gospel, there is no room for superiority or self-importance in it. "Boasting," Paul said, "is excluded" by the singular and universal truth that all of us are guilty as transgressors, just as James said, and that our guilt separates each of us from God.[170] If we remember James's lesson to us, then we will remember that one transgression subjects us to the full damning weight of justice. "If ye have respect to persons," James wrote, "ye commit sin, and are [convicted] of the law as transgressors."[171] Why should I give my own sins more respect than another's? I shouldn't. And to do so turns the judgment upon myself, as James goes on to explain: "For he shall have judgment without mercy, that hath shewed no mercy."[172]

On one occasion, as Jesus dined in a certain house, "many publicans and sinners came and sat down with him and his disciples. And when the Pharisees saw it, they said unto his disciples, Why eateth your Master with publicans and sinners? But when Jesus heard that, he said unto them, They that be whole need not a physician, but they that are sick. But go ye and learn what that meaneth."[173] I marvel at that last line—"But go ye and learn what that meaneth." In other words, he is saying that his words were not merely about those they appeared to be about. He was inviting the Pharisees to go away and reflect both upon his words and upon their own lives, and to discover that they themselves were among the sick who needed the physician! They were focusing merely on the thin outer layer of the gospel and were giving themselves a pass at the deeper level—the level of their hearts. *Go ye and learn,* Jesus was saying, *that you need me as much as any.*

When we shun others because of their particular struggles, we begin to live a wicked lie: We are saying that our own sins are more acceptable than others', and we are therefore implying that they need the Lord's Atonement more than we ourselves do. In these moments, we have joined the Pharisees in questioning why Jesus spent so much time among the "sinners." And to us, too, Jesus is saying, "Go thee, and learn what it meaneth that the whole need not a physician, but they that are sick."

This sin of being a respecter of persons shows itself in many forms. We have looked at two versions in this chapter—the sin of being a respecter of persons based on others' appearance or status, and the sin of being a respecter of persons in terms of sins we accept (our own) and those that we don't. Yet another version of this sin is responsible for much of the tyranny among mankind since the beginning of time. It is the idea that some groups of people are superior to other groups of people—based on their race, for example, or their religion, or their class, or their gender. The notion of such spiritual exceptionalism, which we will explore in the next two chapters, was the creed of the Zoramites. It is our own creed as well whenever and wherever we regard some groups among the fallen children of God as being inherently better (or worse) than others.

14

SUPERIORITY
BY ASSOCIATION

One of the favorite traditions in our stake is our annual "Night of Christmas Choirs." In the beginning, our ward choirs each prepared a number for the evening. Lately, we have moved toward full stake choirs—adult, youth, and Primary age. But no one comes to hear any of these choirs, as marvelous as they always are. No, our building fills to overflowing because of the love and talent of our annual guests, the members of the choir of a prominent Baptist church in our area. Whatever else happens that evening, we always sing "Silent Night" to start with and "O Holy Night" in benediction. In between, our members would revolt if we didn't also hear our friends sing "Amazing Grace" and "Go Tell It on the Mountain." These have become cherished hymns and anthems for us as well.

Every number is spirit-filled, and I'm always struck by how beautifully appropriate it is that these separate bodies of believers come together in praise of our common Lord and Savior during the time of year that reminds us that there should be room for all under any and every roof.

From the first word I ever heard our friends sing in testimony of Jesus, I knew that they loved him as I do. During our latest incarnation of this tradition, I was overwhelmed with the realization that God loves them just as he loves me. Every year, their wonderfully gracious and spirit-filled pastor offers either the invocation or benediction for our meeting. And when he does, he talks with God. I say *with* rather than *to* because there is no doubt in my mind that our Father is listening to and guiding his words as much as he has ever listened to and guided mine. In the middle of his prayer this year, I was hit with this realization: How God must love this good man—who, after all, ministers so faithfully to a large congregation of His children! Since the Lord loves all of his children, he must need and want good leaders and caring ministers in all the churches of the world. He wants all of his children to be uplifted, edified, and brought to Christ. How he must pour out his Spirit upon all who are helping that to happen!

A friend of mine has developed a relationship with a religious leader who has spent the last few decades of his life living with and ministering to the needs of the 30,000 or so people who live on and around an immense rubbish dump in

Manila known as "Smokey Mountain." The name comes from the fact that the waste decomposes at such temperatures that it spontaneously combusts. Conditions there are horrific, as these tens of thousands of people survive only off of what they can find in the dump. How God must ache for these, his suffering children! If his omnipotent eye could be focused only on a finite number of places, surely he would spend more time looking upon and watching over those who are suffering on the Smokey Mountains of the world than he would on his children who, perhaps like you and me, live in what would be historically royal levels of comfort. And how the Lord must love those who minister to and help these suffering ones! How he must pour out his Spirit upon any religious or other leader who puts the needs of the destitute above his own! How he must love the godly souls that fill these needs!

One of the most common phrases in any Latter-day Saint testimony meeting is the declaration that "this is the true church." And so we believe it to be. The priesthood keys that enable the performance of all the necessary ordinances of salvation were restored to the earth through the Prophet Joseph Smith. This is among our testimonies. However, we risk becoming as the Zoramites if we think that being a member of the "true church" makes us the "true people" and others the untrue. With a little reflection, it becomes obvious that one of the foundational teachings of the Church is that mere membership in it does not make one better than anyone else. Jesus' vehement rebuke of the Jews who thought themselves better merely because of their lineage[174] applies to those, as well, who might think themselves better because of their baptism. One might strenuously object to this thought with a question like this: "So are you saying that being baptized a member of the Church isn't necessary?" To which I would answer, "That is not at all what I am saying. Baptism and all the other saving ordinances of the gospel are essential, and the members of the Church in these latter days have been chosen for—that is, charged with—the responsibility of taking those ordinances to the world. But to be chosen for responsibility is not at all to be designated as superior. We have been given an obligation, not a stamp of approval."

Like those I felt superior to on the highway, the Baptist preacher who closed our meeting and the Catholic priest who ministers to the poor of Smokey Mountain may be far truer to God than I am. This is one of the implications of the doctrines of the Lord's true church. What a blessing it is to believe in a gospel that won't allow us to use it as proof of our own goodness relative to others! Jesus could have called the elite to be his apostles, but instead he called the unimpressive, the reviled, and the poor.[175] Jesus could have made the chosen people into the heroes of his parables. But he didn't. He told of priests and Levites passing by on the other side and elevated the reviled Samaritan to the role of savior.[176] Who received his praise for an honest payment of tithe—the one who paid most?

No, the one who paid just barely more than nothing.[177] "God hath chosen the foolish things of the world to confound the wise. . . . And base things of the world, and things which are despised, hath God chosen, yea, and things which are not, to bring to nought things that are."[178] Why does God choose the foolish and the weak and the base and the despised? So that "no flesh," Paul said, "should glory in his presence" but rather "glory in the Lord."[179]

"Every thing which inviteth to do good," Mormon taught, "and to persuade to believe in Christ, is sent forth by the power and gift of Christ; wherefore ye may know with a perfect knowledge it is of God."[180] That suggests, it seems to me, that the good preacher who is teaching others to glory in Christ and to love their neighbors is doing God's work and preparing people to one day accept anything more that needs accepting. "[Since ye now] know the light by which ye may judge," Mormon continued, "see that ye do not judge wrongfully; for with that same judgment which ye judge ye shall also be judged."[181]

Being a Mormon, like being a child of Abraham, brings obligations but not assurances. The temple work we believe is essential for mankind makes this very point: we are entrusted with the responsibility to do it for our fellow man, and our very performance of those ordinances on others' behalf testifies that those who were not members of the Church in this life can nevertheless receive all the blessings of exaltation.

Clearly, when we declare ourselves better based on our

actions or our beliefs, we do so at our own peril. The only comparison that is relevant is our comparison to God, and on that scale all of us are found wanting. If we apply Alma's teaching and "acknowledge [our own] unworthiness before God at all times,"[182] we will keep ourselves from the grave sin of regarding ourselves superior because of our associations with what we regard to be superior things. It is well to be grateful for those associations, but hateful to regard ourselves as exceptional because of them.

15

SUPERIORITY
BY NATURE

A second kind of exceptionalism is at least as damaging as the superiority we might find through either our actions or our religious associations. This second kind of superiority is assumed not as a result of choices made but merely as a fact of nature. Some groups, to use a geological metaphor from the scriptures, might be considered "mountains," and other groups "valleys." This is the sin through the ages that has caused some to believe that one race was inherently inferior to another, for example, or to believe that people in higher classes or castes were inherently superior to those "beneath" them.

Everything Jesus taught was an attack on this idea. All are guilty before him, all must cling to the rod to get to the tree, all must walk the repentant path. He both loves all and leaves no one comfortable. Inviting such comfort would be to invite a spiritual smugness that would put our very salvation at risk. He loves us too much to do this. Each of us must "work out [our] own salvation with fear and trembling" before the Lord.[183] "Every valley shall be filled," Jesus declared, "and every mountain and hill shall be brought low; and the crooked shall be made straight, and the rough ways shall be made smooth."[184] The Lord's work on our hearts pulls down the mountains within us and fills in the valleys. And then we see what was always the truth: we are each of us, as it were, rows in the Lord's fields. He is the husbandman who labors to grow fruit that can be gathered unto God. We, the subjects of that work, are equally in need of his trowel. "Without me," he said, "ye can do nothing."[185]

More and more, however, I hear repeated, even in our church meetings, an idea that invites some to think they need less of the Lord's redeeming work and others need more. These statements are usually made out of love—even out of admiration—but these "compliments," if you will, can be misinterpreted in ways that are misleading and dangerous. This is a delicate issue, susceptible to misunderstanding, so I will try to explain myself carefully and clearly.

I was recently in a high priests group meeting when one of the brethren, his voice breaking, said, "I think women are spiritually superior to men. I know my wife sure is. I don't know what I'd ever do without her." Another brother then chimed in

with an opinion, repeated so often that it has taken on almost
doctrinal status: "I think that's why we have the priesthood
and women don't—they don't need it, but we do in order to
get us to serve and progress." There were agreeing nods around
the room.

I sat with mixed feelings. First, I was filled with gratitude
both for the love of my own wife and for the privilege to attend
church with brethren who were filled with such tender and
loving feelings for *their* companions. The comments troubled
me, however, as well. I thought of the Lord, and of Adam,
Enoch, Abraham, and Jacob. I thought of Moses and Joshua
and Gideon and Samuel. I thought of Elijah and Elisha, Isaiah
and Jeremiah. I thought of Lehi and Nephi, of Mormon and
Moroni. I thought of Peter, of James, and of John. I thought
of Joseph Smith and his loyal brother Hyrum. I thought of the
Presidents of the Church who have followed, and of our pres-
ent-day prophet and members of the Quorum of the Twelve
Apostles. It didn't settle well with me to think that these were
inherently inferior souls, and I sat wondering at how fully ideas
that have no basis in scripture can have become so readily accepted—almost unquestioned, even.

Please do not misunderstand. I think it is a wonderful
thing that a man believes he has married up, even *way* up. But I
think it is wonderful for a woman to feel the same way. Indeed,
the happiest marriages are those in which *both* partners feel
that way, as the feeling that one is lucky to be with his or her

mate is one of the purest expressions of love and surest expressions of devotion. The risk, however, is that we hear such expressions of personal love and gratitude and regard them as statements of doctrine. When this happens, expressions of love can be made into poisons that erode the very foundations of marriage.

Think about it. Even if it were true that one group was spiritually superior to another, the moment someone believed that about himself or herself it would immediately become false. Their arrogance would expose the lie in the spiritual mountain they were making of themselves. So if we preach that women are better than men, what do we invite? First, we invite women to *believe* it—to believe that they *are,* in fact, better than those they have married. What a bitter pill this would be, to believe that one was condemned to be with someone who was inherently inferior! It is a poison pill to personal and marital happiness. Marriages can continue even if only one of the partners feels that he or she is lucky to be married to his or her spouse, but the partnership will not be a full one. And the strains of life, combined with the neglect one feels when married to one who thinks himself or herself superior, can turn the feelings of the other as well. When both partners feel that they are better than their spouses, divorce has already happened in their hearts. The only question remaining is whether they will announce that fact to the public.

The second thing we invite by telling women that they are

better is depression. This is a cruelly ironic outcome, as I think that sometimes people feel moved to tell this to women in order to lift their spirits and make them feel better. But it doesn't work—both because it isn't based on truth and because, even if it were, a number of women know that it wouldn't be true of *them*.

I learned this from a sister in the Church who was a close friend. I had heard that another of our female friends was feeling down about a number of things. I had always loved the struggling woman deeply—in some ways, she had been like a second mother to me. I found her to be one of the most kind and compassionate people I have ever known. So in an effort to lift her spirits, I e-mailed her, telling her what I have just written here—that she is one of the best people I have ever known—and thanking her for being so good to me and to others. My friend, whom I had copied on that note, wrote back and taught me a lesson I will never forget. "Good job, Jim," came the reply. "She will really feel down now."

I was shocked by the note. Had my friend actually read what I had written? I wondered. How could a note so positive and full of thanks as mine possibly make our mutual friend feel worse? I immediately asked her for clarification. It was my friend's reply to this request that opened me to something I had never understood. "Your words will make her feel worse because she doesn't think she's as good as you are describing her to be," she answered. "She knows how she's felt in her life, even at times when she has been doing good, as you described. And she knows she's been wrong to feel those ways. So when you tell her she's great, she knows better, and the gap between what you say about her and what she thinks about herself grows all the wider."

I read the note probably ten times, letting the insight soak in. What was true for this good sister, when hearing praise meant only for her, must be ten times as true of sisters generally when they are told how righteous and loving their whole gender is supposed to be. Many sit and hear that message and know that, while it might be true of others, it certainly isn't true of them. And they now are estranged not only from the men whose presence is implied to be a burden in their lives but also from their fellow sisters whom they now feel to be so very far beyond them. How depressing it must be to be aware of so much personal sinfulness when one is told she is of a gender that is designed to be extra good! That kind of despair, I'm afraid, is too often the result of our well-intentioned efforts to lift.

Another damaging result of this idea, of course, is that it ends up giving men (or whomever else is considered to be the spiritual "valley" at the moment) a pass. "What do you expect?" one who is taught that he is worse might say. "I'm a guy!" Don't laugh. I've heard that plenty—said it a few times myself, in fact. Inferiority is a tremendously powerful justification. Once I've bought into it, I am excused from many things that others more "spiritually gifted" could pull off. I might even convince myself that I am not even as good at repenting as other people are, so why try?

There is an interesting example of this in 1 Nephi 15. "Have ye inquired of the Lord?" Nephi asked Laman and Lemuel. "And they said unto [Nephi]: We have not; for the Lord maketh no such thing known unto us."[186] *We aren't like you are,* they were saying. *We're not as spiritual or as favored. And because we aren't, God doesn't speak to us. So what's the point in praying?*

How much more liberating it is for all of us simply to see the truth: that I am neither inherently better nor inherently worse than others—that I am, in fact, equally fallen and flawed and separated from God. That I need to see how I am wrong before I can get right. That it is a gift that I am seeing my sinfulness. That my hope is through repentance, just as everyone else's hope is—just as my spouse's hope is, for example. *And* that my Savior nevertheless loves me (and my spouse and others) infinitely.

This is not to say that we shouldn't speak kindly of each other. Quite the contrary, when we have no personal need to seem better than others, the compliments will flow freely. Studies show that in healthy relationships, positive comments outnumber negative ones by at least five to one. At first blush, it seems that this means that people don't function well if they are not receiving many more compliments than criticisms.

Whatever truth there may be to this, the greater truth is that people don't function well if they are not *giving* many times more compliments than criticisms, for it is the *giving* of compliments rather than the receiving of them that truly edifies. One who is down is therefore not lifted merely by hearing a compliment but by seeing others in a way that awakens within him or her *the desire to compliment.* For this reason, attempts to lift others that do not invite them to speak better of others but only to think better of themselves usually make matters worse.

One man once told me of the problems he had experienced in his marriage because the brother who had married them told them that he, as the husband, had a priesthood duty to forgive his wife. According to him, his wife had relied upon this teaching as justification for not being forgiving herself.

Now, I have no way of knowing whether this was, in fact, either a true account of what was taught or an honest account of their marriage (and I have reason to doubt the latter). But I can imagine the kinds of problems that could come from such an idea. I have perpetuated this same problem in a number of ways over the years. For example, I have sometimes repeated to newly called bishops in our stake this anecdote: "When calling a new bishop, it has been said that you look for the most dependable, most spiritual, and most charitable person in the ward, and then you call that person's husband as the bishop." Now, that might be a cute thing to say, and a little bit funny, but it strikes me as I think back on those times that it has largely been a gratuitous comment, and that, contrary to intentions, it actually harms both the bishop's wife and the bishop to have heard it.

I remember once hearing President Gordon B. Hinckley say to the men that their wives had taken a terrible risk marrying them. He said it with a smile, and the congregation laughed heartily, but he wasn't joking. The women in our lives really have taken a terrible risk by attaching themselves to us. What is also true, but what a priesthood leader is much less likely to say from the pulpit, is that husbands have taken a terrible risk marrying their wives as well. That is a message that a man will be more reluctant to deliver, as it seems self-serving, but it is equally the truth. No one gender has a corner on righteousness or the Spirit. Each of us needs the Savior equally and infinitely.

Do I believe that men are helped by women to become more than they could be alone? A thousand times, yes. Just as I believe that our gender differences make men helpful to women in precisely the same way. We tweak each other's weaknesses, which allows for individual and mutual growth that would be more difficult to come by otherwise. To invite one gender to think themselves a mountain and the other to consider themselves but a valley is to pit partners against each other and to sow bitterness rather than love. If it is the duty of the man (which I believe it is) to care first and foremost for his wife, it is equally the duty of the wife to care first and foremost for her husband. We tip that balance at the peril of our families.

It seems to me that in wards comprised of healthy families, expressions of love and gratitude for each other would be made in equal proportion in both priesthood and Relief Society lessons and meetings. And neither the men nor the women in the ward would use times they are gathered together—either formally or informally—as opportunities to gripe about, criticize, or look down at their mates. And no group—whether of gender, of race, or of culture—would think itself superior in any way to any other.

Anything that makes me feel better (or worse) than another is darkness; anything that makes me feel one with others is divine. So the natural instinct to try to lift others by helping them to feel good about themselves relative to others is exactly the wrong way to help. True happiness is found not in a belief that I am better but in the obliteration of any need to be.

When this belief is finally rooted out of me, I will begin to do what we will discover in the next chapter is the thing that I most need to do—I will begin to repent of failing to love.

16

WITHHOLDING FORGIVENESS

grew up in Seattle, Washington. We lived in what I would regard to be kind of an idyllic middle-class environment. We never really wanted for anything but, mercifully, weren't surrounded by riches either. Our home was a one-story rambler with a walkout basement. Our two-car carport was half filled with an old eighteen-foot boat we used so little that it actually rusted to the trailer (a big embarrassment, I can assure you, when, after many years, we tried to launch it in front of an incredulous crowd at the marina). The other half of the carport was always occupied by a station wagon of some sort (yellow with brown wood paneling being my personal favorite).

From the facing on the roof of the carport hung a basketball hoop. Placed about nine feet high directly beneath the basket, it was eleven feet high from twenty feet away—the angle of the driveway making for a wonderful home court advantage. It is impossible to calculate how many hours I spent shooting baskets on that court. It is also impossible to calculate how important it was for my development—both in sports and in life—to have spent many of those hours playing against Mark and Dave Bean, my Church-member neighbors, who were three and four years older than I was. Both of them gifted athletes, for some reason they treated me as if I were their age, and we spent hours and days and likely years together playing basketball, or football, or baseball, or Ping-Pong, or anything else involving projectiles of one sort or another. The Beans were two of the most influential and best friends of my childhood. But that doesn't mean we didn't have our moments.

One day, when I was still quite young—perhaps nine years old or so—the three of us were playing a game on their back patio. It involved a wooden top that you launched into a wooden box that was arranged into compartments or rooms. In each room were placed miniature wooden bowling pins. The more difficult pins to reach had higher point values. The object was to make the top spin fast enough that it would frantically dart from one room to the next and knock down as many pins, for as many points, as possible. We had played this game many times, often as a brief diversion from Ping-Pong or some other activity. It was still quite early on this particular summer day, probably around nine A.M. or so, when I took my turn with the top. I gripped the string tightly and yanked it with everything I had. But then, instead of hearing the tight rumble of the whirling top, there was silence. The top had evaporated into thin air. We looked around and at each other. *Where had it gone?* After a moment it was obvious that instead of propelling the top onto the playing surface, I had somehow launched it skyward.

"Hey, Ferrell," one of the Bean boys said, "you lost our top!"

"I didn't mean to," I defended myself. "I don't know what happened."

"You better find it or we're going to beat you up!" the other one threatened.

"But I don't know what happened!" I said, bursting into tears.

"We don't care, you'd better find it anyway."

For a few minutes I wandered aimlessly around our adjoining yards. Nothing. Dave and Mark were looking as well, but they too came up empty.

"I can't find it," I lamented.

"Well, you'd better," they insisted.

Their earlier threat still hung in the air between us. "But what if I *can't?*"

"You'd better."

At that, I dashed back to the safety of my house and locked the door.

So began more than a year of estrangement from my neighbors and best friends. We didn't play with each other anymore. In fact, we barely spoke, and when we did, it was in threatening tones. I was terrified to walk to school at the same time they did, varying my schedule unnaturally just to avoid them. Looking back, I can remember that we all applied a kind of odd truce during our church meetings—we still didn't speak much, but the violent undertones, at least, appeared to take a Sabbath. But come Monday, it was war again. If a ball of mine crossed the property line into their yard, they kicked it over a neighbor's fence. When they weren't looking, I returned the favor. Much more became lost than the single top that had started all the trouble.

More than a year went by like this—until the day my mother found the top while working in our garden. It wasn't but thirty minutes later that the Bean boys were on my doorstep asking if I wanted to play some basketball.

Oh, to be a kid again, when heartache and grudges can be let go of in an instant! Unfortunately, somehow, somewhere, we come to prize our grudges, and we clutch to them and the lies they tell us despite all evidence or "found tops" to the contrary. Even worse, the "lost tops" aren't always found. What then? Are we then compelled to resent and war against each other forever?

As with most questions, the clearest and truest answer can be found by pondering the Savior and his offering. The

Lord effectively experienced all the "lost tops" in the history of the world, most of which were never found. And by proxy, he suffered for us all the mistreatment and heartache that followed those and all other experiences in mortality. Before we continue to rage against those we feel have hurt us, perhaps we should ponder over his response to the suffering he experienced on *our* behalf. His response, despite suffering that infinitely dwarfs our own, is to lovingly take us in his arms and work eternally to redeem and to sanctify us. And why? Because he wants to be with us, and he wants us to enjoy all that he has! How do our own responses to suffering compare to this?

One evening, my wife said something to me that I thought was unfair, and I took offense at it. In the instant I took offense, I began pulling away. My words no longer flowed. My thoughts became troubled. I no longer wanted to linger in her presence but instead retreated behind plastered walls that resembled the barriers I had erected in my heart. The evening became artificially silent—voices no longer filled the air, but the atmosphere around us nevertheless crackled with felt insult and accusation. I waited for the apology I thought I was owed, unaware that my waiting—the feeling that an apology was required before I would be willing to forgive and once again extend my love—was just as off-putting as the act that I had taken offense at in the first place! By my own internal logic, my wife would have as much reason to wait for my apology as I had to wait for hers. And so we each waited, and waited, and waited, every moment making it less likely that anyone would ever apologize for anything.

Had you been a guest in our home that night, you might have felt to grab my collar and say, "Grow up, Jim! Let it go! Forgive her—she didn't mean anything by what she said. And even if she did, forgive her anyway!" Your counsel would have been good and wise. But it would have been unlikely to help. Why? Because in that moment and all others like it, I am misunderstanding what is meant by "forgiveness."

The word itself sets us up for misunderstanding. To "forgive" someone sounds like such a gallant act—a favor dispensed upon another despite his or her despicable mistreatment or thoughtlessness. And if I view it this way, I will be tempted to wait for some act of contrition on the other's part that I would be willing to accept in exchange for the love I am withholding. In the story I just shared, the price I had placed on receipt of my love was an apology. That price was increasing moment by moment, meaning that I was withholding my love more and more as my wife persisted in not apologizing! I was speaking less, looking at her less, being with her less. If she too took offense, then her demanded price would increase each moment as well. Each of us would insist that we were willing to forgive, but we would be blind to the deal we were actually offering: that we would be willing to extend our love to the other once again only after that person paid the price our offended selves had set for it.

Our idea of forgiveness in such cases is a small and miserly and decrepit thing. It must be earned, we insist, blind to our own unwillingness to pay the purchase price. We have sucked all the light and divinity from the redeeming act of forgiveness and are using it instead as a crass currency of exchange. As if love must, or can, be purchased. Does Christ withhold his love from us? Does he not, rather, come to us, and bid us come to him, "without price"?[187]

Any withholding of love is itself a sin.[188] So to have held it back on account of what another has done is itself an act for which we must repent. Sometimes, the act that precipitates this repentance is for the one who has harmed the other to come and beg the harmed party's "forgiveness." I think it may be partly for this reason that we call the aggrieved party's act an act of forgiveness. But make no mistake, when I as the harmed party respond to this request by giving up my resentment and my grudge, what I am doing is repenting—repenting of my failing to love. *Forgiveness* is simply the word we use to describe this kind of *repentance*.[189]

This kind of repentance—the repentance that we call forgiveness—is the most crucial kind of repentance of all. The Lord teaches us that if we don't repent of withholding forgiveness, then we ourselves will not be able to receive the mercy that we need in order to be redeemed. Consider, for example, the Lord's Prayer. One element in the prayer is not like the other elements, and it is my belief that the Lord uttered this prayer precisely so that we would see and learn from the element that is different. See if you can pick it out.

> Our Father which art in heaven, Hallowed be thy name. Thy kingdom come. Thy will be done in earth, as it is in heaven. Give us this day our daily bread. And forgive us our debts, as we forgive our debtors. And lead us not into temptation, but deliver us from evil: For thine is the kingdom, and the power, and the glory, for ever. Amen.[190]

Do you notice the element in this prayer that is different from the others? The Lord puts a condition on one and only one item in the prayer: "Forgive us our debts," he prays, "*as we forgive our debtors.*"[191] The forgiveness of our eternal debts, the Lord is saying, depends on our repenting of the sin of failing to love those who have mistreated us. Just so we don't miss that lesson, the Lord immediately tells us that this is the very point we are to get from this prayer: "For if ye forgive men their trespasses," he explains after closing the prayer, "your heavenly Father will also forgive you: But if ye forgive not men their trespasses, neither will your Father forgive your trespasses."[192]

If we have not been forgiving of others, then we are in urgent need of repentance. For, as James says, "he shall have judgment without mercy, that hath shewed no mercy."[193] It will be of no profit to us, he adds, to have faith in the Lord's mercy

117

for us if we ourselves have not also shown merciful works to others.[194] Such faith, James declares, "is dead, being alone."[195]

Pride would have me stay alone, waiting for others to earn my companionship. The Lord, on the other hand, beckons that we who don't deserve *his* companionship nevertheless join him. Whether we accept this invitation or not will depend on two things. First, it will depend on whether we will rejoice in being joined to him *with others*—in particular, with those we are currently waiting to forgive.

The other matter, of course, is whether we feel we can join him ourselves. As we shall discuss in the next chapter, the matter of forgiving oneself is also commonly misunderstood. Here, as well, our normal inclinations can lead us astray.

17

FORGIVING ONESELF

One of the most common expressions I hear these days is the idea of how important it is, and how difficult, to forgive oneself. It seems beyond question in most people's minds that this is a real and legitimate problem that needs a real and earnest solution. But the scriptures give me pause. If forgiving oneself is such a real and important need, then why is it not mentioned anywhere in all the standard works? Why did Jesus never mention it, even when it would have been obvious by modern standards to do so—such as to the woman taken in adultery? He didn't say, "Woman, forgive yourself," even though the circumstances were such that she might struggle mightily with what she had done. Rather, he told her to "Go, and sin no more."[196]

Nor did Jesus help Peter to forgive himself when his faith wavered on the water. Quite to the contrary, he gently rebuked him: "O thou of little faith, wherefore didst thou doubt?"[197] Likewise, Jesus told Peter that he would deny him three times before the morning,[198] a prophecy that he knew would leave Peter reeling when it was fulfilled.[199] He apparently didn't, however, feel the need at all to soften the blow or to counsel Peter to let it go and forgive himself. Nor did the angel tell Alma to quit beating himself up over what he had done, to forgive himself and move on.[200] And neither the Lord nor King Benjamin told the diligent, commandment-keeping people who had gathered to the temple in Zarahemla to get up from their knees and forgive themselves.[201] No, as we discussed in the previous chapter, we are not in the forgiving business, even of ourselves. There is One who actually forgives, and that isn't us.[202] Rather, we are to be in the repenting business. And in repenting, we discover the immensity of God's love for us—a love we ourselves, perhaps, might have departed from for a time, but that we will feel in abundance the moment we approach the Lord in "meekness, and lowliness of heart."[203] As counterintuitive as it may sound, in the cases where we are struggling to forgive ourselves, what is needed is not forgiveness of self but more repentance.

"But repentance from what?" one might object. "Am I not already 'meek and lowly in heart' when I'm struggling to forgive myself?" Here is the crux of the matter. What seems meek and humble in this case is pride in disguise, as we discussed in chapter 10. Think about it: Is it meek and lowly to believe that whether or not God forgives me, I cannot rest until I can forgive myself? Is that not pride of the highest order?

When we feel that we are struggling to forgive ourselves, we are usually upset at ourselves for something we have done that we think was bad, or embarrassing, or faithless, or perhaps reprehensible. We struggle with the idea that we ever did such a thing (often, although not necessarily, in part because we feel terrible that others might know that we did it). Our own concept of self has been injured, so we both feel the need and experience the difficulty of "forgiving ourselves." But it's a revealing thing that we feel the need to forgive ourselves only when our self-concept feels injured. This reality implies two possibilities: Either the injured self is telling me the truth and I need to find a way to forgive myself, or else I need to repent of the self-concept that makes forgiving myself seem like the issue.

One of my favorite passages in the scriptures is Nephi's lament in the fourth chapter of Second Nephi about his own personal struggles with sinfulness. He was in the kind of depressed state of mind that might lead a person to the conclusion that he needed to forgive himself. But forgiving himself was not Nephi's answer at all. Nor, his story implies, should it be ours.

Notwithstanding the great goodness of the Lord,
in showing me his great and marvelous works, [Nephi

wrote,] my heart exclaimeth: O wretched man that I
am! Yea, my heart sorroweth because of my flesh; my
soul grieveth because of mine iniquities. I am encompassed about, because of the temptations and sins
which do so easily beset me. And when I desire to
rejoice, my heart groaneth because of my sins.[204]

This sounds very much like a person one might counsel to
forgive himself, doesn't it? But Nephi turned in a completely
different direction. Instead of turning to himself, he began a
turn to the Lord. He began by turning in remembrance to the
great mercies that the Lord had shown him over the years.
These mercies are detailed from verses 20 through 25. This
remembrance awakened within him a realization of a need for
repentance that he, in his despair, had been missing:

Oh then, if I have seen so great things, if the Lord
in his condescension unto the children of men hath
visited men in so much mercy, why should my heart
weep and my soul linger in the valley of sorrow, and
my flesh waste away, and my strength slacken, because
of mine afflictions? And why should I yield to sin,
because of my flesh? Yea, why should I give way to
temptations, that the evil one have place in my heart to
destroy my peace and afflict my soul? Why am I angry
because of mine enemy? Awake, my soul! No longer
droop in sin. Rejoice, O my heart, and give place no

more for the enemy of my soul. Do not anger again
because of mine enemies. Do not slacken my strength
because of mine afflictions.[205]

After Nephi's mind turned to Christ, the antidote for his
despair turned out not to be some self-centered forgiveness of
himself but a new resolve to repent. This turn away from himself and to Christ became complete as he turned to Him for the
help he would need on this deeper path of repentance. Notice
in the following passage how many times he refers to and ap-
peals to the Lord, recognizing that what he needs is from *Him*
and not from himself.

O Lord, I will praise thee forever; yea, my soul will
rejoice in thee, my God, and the rock of my salvation.
O Lord, wilt *thou* redeem my soul? Wilt *thou* deliver me
out of the hands of mine enemies? Wilt *thou* make me
that I may shake at the appearance of sin? May the gates
of hell be shut continually before me, because my heart
is broken and my spirit is contrite! O Lord, wilt *thou* not
shut the gates of thy righteousness before me, that I may
walk in the path of the low valley, that I may be strict in
the plain road! O Lord, wilt *thou* encircle me around in
the robe of thy righteousness! O Lord, wilt *thou* make
a way for mine escape before mine enemies! Wilt *thou*
make my path straight before me! Wilt *thou* not place a

stumbling block in my way—but that *thou* wouldst clear my way before me, and hedge not up my way.[206]

Rejoicing now in the Lord rather than feeling depressed that he cannot rejoice in himself, Nephi expresses what he has learned from his journey into personal despair and back: that there is no way back from self-loathing by relying on the "arm of flesh"—which is to say, upon oneself.

O Lord, I have trusted in thee, and I will trust in thee forever. I will not put my trust in the arm of flesh; for I know that cursed is he that putteth his trust in the arm of flesh. Yea, cursed is he that putteth his trust in man or maketh flesh his arm.[207]

The lifting help of forgiveness is the Lord's, not ours, to give. And to think otherwise is to render the Lord's forgiveness insufficient and secondary to our own.

Jesus showed us the way in his exchange with the woman taken in adultery. The scribes and Pharisees brought the woman before him in another attempt to entrap him in the web of the law. "Master," they said, feigning respect, "this woman was taken in adultery, in the very act. Now Moses in the law commanded us, that such should be stoned: but what sayest thou?"[208] Jesus didn't immediately respond, but crouched down and wrote with his finger in the dirt, as if he hadn't heard them. The scripture says that they "continued asking him"—they badgered him—whereupon he stood up and uttered one of the most oft-quoted lines in all of holy writ. "He that is without sin among you, let him first cast a stone at her."[209] He didn't deny what the law said, but he taught them what Paul and James later wrote about—that the law catches and condemns all of us, as all of us are convicted as transgressors of the law and are therefore, effectively, guilty of all. One by one, the men who stood round were "convicted by their own conscience" and left, one guilty soul at a time.

Jesus' statement to these men was meant not only for them. He was teaching a principle—a truth that was crucial for the woman to understand as well, a truth that those of us who might be struggling in the misguided quest to forgive ourselves have not yet fully understood. *All* are guilty under the law, a guilt that separates us from God. What does it mean to forgive ourselves when we are, in effect, "guilty of all"? Clearly, the power of such forgiveness is not within us; the guilty cannot render themselves innocent. Only the judge—in this case, the great and Eternal Judge[210]—can do that.

So "forgiving oneself" is a misnomer. We, ourselves, are not the aggrieved party, and we, as the guilty, cannot render ourselves innocent. We are just feeling bad for having done bad, and we want to find a way to quit grinding our own faces in the sand. And here, Jesus' final words to the woman, in combination with his teaching that *all* are guilty, provides the release we are looking for but in all the wrong places: "Woman,

where are those thine accusers?" he asked. "Hath no man condemned thee?" She answered, "No man, Lord." Then Jesus
said, "Neither do I condemn thee: go, and sin no more."[211]

Think about those words: *Neither do I condemn thee.* If she
understood who it was that was telling her this, she would be
released forever from any perceived need to forgive herself. For
this was the great and Eternal Judge himself—our "advocate"
with the Father[212]—telling her that he did not condemn her.
And if *he* didn't, then why should she still feel the need to
condemn herself? The guilt we feel in our hearts can be taken
from us only "through the merits of [the] Son."[213] It is the ad-
versary who tries to get us to worry about forgiving ourselves.

"To day shalt thou be with me in paradise," Jesus reassured
the thief who hung humbly and repentantly next to him.[214] His
promises to us are not frustrated by our sins. Rather, they can
be frustrated only by our lacking a desire to repent of those
sins. "Go and sin no more" was the Lord's direction to the
woman to live a repentant life—a life we are diverted from as
we search in vain for a forgiveness that we cannot receive from
ourselves.

18

GREAT EXPECTATIONS

My family owns a most imperfect yet remarkable dog. He was Santa's gift to our oldest child when our son was eight years old. The dog, a springer spaniel named Oakley, is now himself eight. At times, I have found him to be frustrating and odd. For one thing, he is constantly digging up our yard. Just as we fix the damage in one area he rotates to another. We've been chasing his holes for most of his life. And among his odd quirks is that he absolutely will not play fetch. He is as anxious to fly after a ball as any dog I have seen, but he then runs away with his "kill" to gnaw at it. When you try to retrieve it from him, he flees. In every case, he wants to keep his toy to himself. In fact, when we give him special chew toys, he runs off and buries them somewhere in the yard, never to be found again, even by him. It's the same story when we give him a bone. Off it goes to some soon-forgotten grave.

In the early days, we discussed giving Oakley away, but ultimately we couldn't do it. Today we wouldn't let him go for the whole world. Why? Because he has become our teacher.

If you were to visit our home, you would see Oakley sitting at our back door, anxiously peering through the glass. He must spend ninety percent of his waking hours in that same spot and position, patiently waiting for us to join him. No matter how long he waits for personal attention and companionship— whether hours or sometimes even days—he seems to love us all the same. No matter how long he has waited—sometimes in the extreme cold, and other times without food—I can discern no change in his demeanor toward us. There is no hint of demand, of complaint, or even of expectation in him. There is only hope. Hope that cannot be quenched by anything we do or fail to do with or for him.

A few years after we got Oakley, one of our daughters wanted her own puppy, and we purchased a second springer— this one a wily little imp named Oreo. Oreo was brilliant and strong willed, quick as a cat, with eyes that searched for mischief. He gobbled down sizzling hamburgers from off the grill, nipped at you when you passed by him, and generally treated Oakley roughly. When he was a young puppy, I thought his rough ways with Oakley were cute—just learning his limits, I thought. But he didn't seem to find limits that restrained him.

As he got older, he mangled Oakley's legs and ears and frequently caused Oakley to bleed. All the while, Oakley stoically continued looking for us through the glass.

When we went out in the backyard with the two of them, Oreo always darted to cut Oakley off when Oakley approached us for some love and attention. Although much younger, Oreo had crowned himself the alpha dog, and Oakley had consented to it. He waited in the background while Oreo received attention from us and only afterward nudged his way forward for the same. I felt bad for Oakley. But part of me just wanted him to toughen up and not to let Oreo dominate him.

One day in the middle of all this, the dogs got out of our yard and ran into the backyard of a neighbor, drawn there by a swift-moving stream and the laughter of children at play. Oreo, fearless and impetuous as always, dove headlong into the water. This was the first time he had ever tried to swim, and he struggled mightily. Fear showed in his eyes, possibly for the first time, as he was being swept uncontrollably downstream. I marvel at what happened next. Oakley dove in after him. He paddled furiously to reach his tormentor. Oreo grabbed at him and struggled to pull the front of his body onto Oakley's back. With his rider safely aboard, Oakley paddled them both to the safety of the bank.

When my daughter told me this story, I was filled with wonder at this dog. How was it that this mistreated, neglected, and taken-for-granted canine had developed such character?

I began to wonder what his human equivalent might be. Imagine, for example, waiting minute by minute, hour by hour, and day by day for others in my life to do what I would like them to do—to show me kindness, for example, or attention, or love, or to do what I've asked them to do. Or imagine being systematically mistreated—unappreciated, for example, or unhelped, or ignored, or pushed aside. And then I realized that this often *is* our condition and situation in life. Our companions, no matter who they are, will frequently fail to do what we would like them to do or to act as we would ideally like to them to act. And our children may systematically fail to help or to appreciate us. When I realized this, the question that made Oakley my teacher came into my heart: In dealing with these and other challenges, how do we compare to this dog?

Do we, like Oakley, view others only with hope and gratitude? Or do we rather view others with a critical eye, demanding that they be different than they are? If, like Oakley, we are filled only with hope, we will be able to feel gratitude for others notwithstanding their faults. If, on the other hand, we feel entitled, we condemn ourselves to a resented life and will feel embittered toward those whom we have been called to love and to cherish.

Oakley still has the same quirks and "faults" as he's always had, but we are not troubled by them anymore. Would we prefer it if he quit digging? Yes. Would we sometimes like him to play fetch? Yes. But these and his other quirks don't keep us from loving him and being grateful for him. Why? Here again, Oakley has been our teacher. I believe we are not troubled by his faults because *he is not troubled by ours*. There is no up-ness in him. Despite the countless ways that we have been less-than-ideal companions for him, he still hopes to be with us and thinks no less of us even if we keep ourselves from him for longer than more thoughtful people might. His gratitude has won us over. How can we reject one who loves so freely?

The Apostle Paul had some things to say about being like Oakley. While imprisoned,[215] he wrote: "I have learned, in whatsoever state I am, therewith to be content."[216] "Content with prison?" one might ask, incredulously. Yes. "With bonds?" Yes. "Then you're doomed!" the questioner might respond. "Doomed to a life of bondage!" But the inquirer would be mistaken. Paul remained free, despite the prison walls around him. The Romans could lock up his body, but they could imprison Paul's soul only with his consent—consent that Paul's contentment denied them. Contented, Paul remained free from the constant disappointment created by ex-pectation. Nothing anyone else did or failed to do could exert control over his heart. Despite his less-than-ideal situation, he, like Oakley, remained free—free from the bondage of resent-ment and blame. He could remain filled with hope, no present deprivation robbing him of a moment's worth of happiness.

I am aware, of course, that some people live in very diffi-cult circumstances. Some face challenges that seem too much even to hear about, much less to bear. Others have been on the receiving end of unthinkable mistreatment. *What if I find myself in such a circumstance?* one might object. *Am I simply to remain, as Paul suggested, content? Am I simply to wait obediently, like Oakley, no matter the mistreatments that come my way? That seems like madness!*

I have wrestled with this same question and with some difficult circumstances of my own. That wrestle caused me to want to explore this very issue in writing. I wanted to detail a set of considerations that might tell a person when he or she might be justified, for example, in choosing to run from certain situations. With every attempt to write on that topic, however, inspiration fled from me. After many attempts, I finally came to this realization: There may be times when one no longer needs to turn the other cheek, or when the cloak no longer needs to be lent,[217] or when one has waited long enough at the door, but such direction can only be given to a person individually and specifically by the Spirit. It appears that even the writers of the scriptures were not authorized to write of acceptable exceptions to these outward rules of long-suffering love, as neither the Savior nor his representatives appear ever to have stated any exemptions. Upon reflection, I believe the reason for this is clear: If there were exceptions to these rules, I would have written myself into them a thousand times over—whenever I met up against circumstances that I thought were unfair!

On the other hand, the scriptures do contain examples of

times when the *Spirit* whispered that it was time to leave certain situations. This is what happened, for example, when the Spirit finally told Nephi that it was time to escape from his brothers.[218] Had the scriptures contained exceptions to long-suffering love, Nephi probably would have written himself into those exceptions years earlier. Had he done so, he would never have obtained the repentance he found as he pleaded heavenward in the chapter before he was told to go[219]—a level of humility and repentance that his hardship, in part, made possible. And we, then, would not have learned from his learning. His own exception-finding would have invited us to exempt ourselves from these laws of long-suffering as well.

But Nephi didn't do this. And he didn't because the scriptures kept him bound to his brothers until the Spirit said it was enough. The outward rules bind us to the difficult path, a fact that helps to keep us in situations that our own sinfulness would have compelled us to abandon long before. This forbearance under difficult circumstances ends up teaching us and others more about love and repentance than any reality we might have willed for ourselves. Then, in the midst of our faithfulness, if it becomes needful for us to leave a circumstance, the Spirit can come individually to us, as it did to Nephi, and give direction that no source within this world can give.

Whether one, like Paul, is confined to prison, or, like Oakley, is still waiting at the door, "the peace of God, which passeth all understanding," Paul wrote from his prison, "shall keep your hearts and minds through Christ Jesus."[220] From this prison he shared the secret for such peace and such contentment and such hope, whatever one's circumstance: "Whatsoever things are true," he wrote, "whatsoever things are honest, whatsoever things are just, whatsoever things are pure, whatsoever things are lovely, whatsoever things are of good report; *if there be any virtue, and if there be any praise, think on these things.*"[221] If there be *anything* virtuous in a person or in a circumstance, Paul is saying, we should think on that single virtuous thing rather than upon the litany of the person's faults or upon the myriad difficulties of life. If there is *anything* lovely or of good report or praiseworthy around us, we are to think on *those* things rather than upon the infinite list of dishonest, impure, ugly, and mean-spirited injustices that could absorb our attention and consume our hearts. Do this, he is telling us, whether from within bondage or without, and we shall remain contented, hope-filled, grateful, free. And we shall therefore be in a position to hear and heed any whisperings of the Spirit that come our way.

One might object that it is a dishonest and even dangerous thing to think only on the good of a person who is bad. To which I would say that I reject the premise. Only One who has ever lived was entirely good, and I would be surprised if there has ever been one who has been entirely bad. It is my own sin, not another's, to see only bad even where there is good. If a person feared to see the good in another because they worried that to do so would expose them more fully to the bad, I would suggest that honesty about a person's strengths does not mean that I would not also see that person's weaknesses. Paul is just inviting us not to snuff the light from our vision and from our hearts by allowing ourselves to see only another's faults. He is begging us not to enter prisons of our own making.

Shed the expectations and the demands and the criticisms that too often consume us, Paul says, and "the God of peace shall be with you."[222]

Just as he is with Oakley.

PART FOUR

THE CONFESSIONAL LIFE

19

INSPIRING HONESTY

Over the last few chapters, perhaps you have come to worry about problems you didn't know you had. And perhaps these problems, when added to those you know all too well, add up to too much to bear. Perhaps you have realized, for example, that you are sometimes a "respecter of persons." Or that you are susceptible to feeling yourself inferior or superior to others. Or perhaps there are places in your life where you are struggling to forgive (that is, to repent of failing to love). Or perhaps you obsess over forgiving yourself, or you feel compelled to lay frequent demands and heavy expectations on others and feel constantly disappointed as a result. Or perhaps you feel your heart lagging behind even when you are doing good. If you feel challenged in any of these ways, you and I have much in common.

And perhaps we share as well a yearning for the "freer sky" G. K. Chesterton spoke of—a life lived outside of the tiny and tawdry theatre that has too often been our abode. Stepping out of the imprisonment of that theatre and into the light happens in the moment we stop acting and begin living—in the moment we put down our masks, take off our costumes, and love and trust others enough to begin offering them nothing more, and nothing less, than who we are. When we do this, we begin living in a "confessional" kind of way, our hearts inclined toward God and toward one another—a way of living that is the antidote to the up-ness we have been exploring. I would like to explore this antidote with you through the remainder of this book.

Earlier I mentioned that "the Psalm of Nephi" in 2 Nephi 4 is one of my favorite passages of scripture. I love it because of how Nephi exposed his weakness and his struggles to us. "O wretched man that I am!" he lamented. "My soul grieveth because of mine iniquities. I am encompassed about, because of the temptations and the sins which do so easily beset me. And when I desire to rejoice, my heart groaneth because of my sins."[223] He wrote specifically of the difficulty he had controlling his emotions, chastising himself for giving the enemy of his soul power over him unto anger.[224] He didn't have to share any of this with us; after all, he was the one writing the record.

But he shared it anyway. He chose to expose his challenges to us. He confessed his weaknesses to the whole world. And I love him for it.

I am inspired as well by Alma, who spoke to his sons of his own sinfulness—conversations that were private and could have been kept that way.[225] He, too, as the author of the record, chose to confess those details to the whole world. This was a continuation of what he did immediately after his call to repentance by the angel. The record says that he and the sons of Mosiah "traveled throughout all the land of Zarahemla, and among all the people who were under the reign of king Mosiah, zealously striving to repair all the injuries which they had done to the church, *confessing all their sins,* and publishing all the things which they had seen."[226] Alma absolutely did not shrink from painting himself and his actions in the worst possible light, using the most reprehensible act known in our language as an analogy for what he had done: "Yea, and I had murdered many of his children," he wrote, "or rather led them away unto destruction."[227] He didn't have to write that or to publicly characterize his actions that way, but he did. He didn't have to write that "so great had been my iniquities, that the very thought of coming into the presence of God did rack my soul with inexpressible horror," but he did. He didn't have to expose his sins and weaknesses to us the way he did, but he did so nonetheless. And I love him for it.

I am inspired as well by Amulek. I love how he described

himself to his people: "I never have known much of the ways of the Lord," he began, "and his mysteries and marvelous power. I said I never had known much of these things; but behold, I mistake, for I have seen much of his mysteries and his marvelous power; yea, even in the preservation of the lives of this people. Nevertheless, I did harden my heart, for I was called many times and I would not hear; therefore I knew concerning these things, yet I would not know; therefore I went on rebelling against God, in the wickedness of my heart."[228] He didn't have to say that about himself! He could have elected to introduce himself in many different ways—ways that might have emphasized his high standing in the community and his success in business.[229] But he didn't. He chose instead to elaborate his struggles in the gospel—struggles that perhaps might resemble some of our own. And I love him for it.

Amulek's honesty reminds me of the honesty of the father who desperately wanted Jesus to heal his son. "If thou canst believe," Jesus said to the man, "all things are possible to him that believeth."[230] And "straightway," the scripture says, "the father of the child cried out, and said with tears, Lord, I believe." And then this humble father, perhaps pausing and bowing his head, made an admission that fills my heart with love and admiration for him. It was something he didn't have to say—something, in fact, that he knew might keep from him the very miracle he so wanted. "Help thou mine unbelief," he pleaded.[231] Oh, how I love him for that! What seemed an admission of unbelief was in actual fact an expression of the deepest kind of faith. Upon this confession, Jesus cast from the boy the spirit that had torn at him since his infancy. And "Jesus took him by the hand, and lifted him up; and he arose."[232]

Another favorite story is the account of the Lamanite king who took upon himself the name of "Anti-Nephi-Lehi"[233] (and whose people were then referred to as "the people of Anti-Nephi-Lehi"[234]). I am inspired by his honest account of his own and his people's history: "I thank my great God that he has given us a portion of his Spirit to soften our hearts," he said, "that we have been convinced of our sins, and of the many murders which we have committed. And I also thank my God, yea, my great God, that he hath granted unto us that we might repent of these things, and also that he hath forgiven us of those our many sins and murders which we have committed, and taken away the guilt from our hearts, through the merits of his Son."[235] So humble was this man that he didn't trust his own or his people's ability to retain the forgiveness they had received for their shedding of blood unless they buried their weapons so deep in the earth that they couldn't retrieve them even if they wanted to.[236]

Many theories have been shared about why the king took the rather odd name of Anti-Nephi-Lehi upon himself and, by extension, upon his people. The record does not give us a definitive reason. I would like to add an additional possibility that perhaps has not been considered before: Perhaps this name seemed suitable because it was a humble expression of who they had been—a name that would forever remind them of, and confess to others, a sinful history that they never wanted to repeat. "We are the people who used to war against Nephi and Lehi, progenitors toward whom our hearts have been mercifully softened, and whom we now revere." If so, their name, like the burying of their weapons of war, was "a testimony to God, and also to men," of the past sins that they were committed to never repeat.[237] They didn't have to be so public about their sins. They certainly didn't have to brand their sins upon them, as it were, through application of a name that kept those sins ever in their memories. But it seems that they did. And I love them for it.

I am inspired by the Apostle Paul for similar reasons. This great man, this missionary and Apostle for Christ, frequently wrote of his own challenges. "For I know that in me," he wrote, "dwelleth no good thing: for to will is present with me; but how to perform that which is good I find not. For the good that I would I do not: but the evil which I would not, that I do."[238] He didn't have to write that! But he did. I love him for not needing to have us think that he was perfect, or close to perfect, unreachable by the common man. Elsewhere he wrote, "I am the least of the apostles, that am not meet to be called an apostle, because I persecuted the church of God."[239] In another letter, he said that he regarded himself not just the least of the apostles but the least of all saints![240] And to Timothy, he wrote,

"Christ Jesus came into the world to save sinners; *of whom I am chief.*"[241]

What is interesting to me is that none of this confessing makes us think any less of these people. On the contrary, their openness and honesty regarding their challenges make us think *more* of them. They become our favorite of all people.

I have learned this lesson over many years of working with those who are struggling to come back to the Church, and from being blessed by the honest and sometimes public confessions of those who struggle with certain aspects of our faith. In a recent church meeting I attended, a faithful young sister spoke of her own struggle with aspects of her testimony. And yet there she stood, sharing that struggle with us, her own presence and humble admission an example of a most perseverant faith.

Some of the most edifying meetings I have ever attended are firesides provided by the Church's "Addiction Mission," where those who have struggled with various addictions in their lives tell their stories and then testify of their belief. Similarly, some of my choicest and most personally meaningful moments with the Spirit have been when individuals in Church disciplinary proceedings have honestly and contritely confessed their struggles and have simultaneously expressed their overwhelming love for the Savior and for those they have hurt in their lives, hoping that perhaps there might still be a future for them in the kingdom. The Spirit is never stronger than in the presence of such open and honest confession.

Why are such confessions so edifying and inspiring? I believe for two main reasons. Paul wrote about the first in First Timothy: "Howbeit for this cause I obtained mercy, that in me first Jesus Christ might shew forth all longsuffering, for a pattern to them which should hereafter believe on him to life everlasting."[242] In other words, stories such as those of Paul and Nephi, Alma and Amulek, Anti-Nephi-Lehi and the father who pleaded for help for his unbelief, and the stories of those who share their struggles with us today, are powerful and uplifting because they manifest the miracle that the Lord can work in us. But this is true only because these people first confessed their faults to us. Had they not, there would be no miracle to see. If we did not know their struggles, their stories would not inspire us and give us hope.

The second reason why confession is so inspiring is because moments of heartfelt confession are the moments of greatest meekness and lowliness of heart.[243] To any who might wonder how the Spirit could attend those who are in the throes of sin, I would say, we *all* are in the throes of sin. The question for us, and the issue upon which the presence of the Spirit depends, is whether we are in the throes of *repentance.* I love all the humble, broken, contrite, confessing souls who have taught me that truth. Their honest contrition and heartfelt repentance have been invitations for me to walk in the direction they are resolutely traveling—toward the Lord—and to do so with a heart that is broken and contrite enough to allow him to lift me.

At a funeral I recently attended, a young woman sang the most stirring rendition of "How Great Thou Art" that I have ever heard. She had the voice of an angel. I sat basking in the spirit that she was pulling down from the heavens. And then, halfway through, touched both by the spirit of the moment and by the message she was delivering, her voice began to waver. Only a moment earlier she had been projecting sound that traveled all the way to the rear of the hall and back. Suddenly, her words were barely escaping her lips. The brilliant instrument that was her voice began to squeak. She could squeeze out only every fifth word or so. The spirit that overcame her washed over the congregation in an instant, and her quiet words were suddenly accompanied by a symphony of sniffing. Overcome as all others were, even though I had never met the deceased, I sat stunned in the realization that the last half of her number was even more beautiful than the first. How was it that the song became better as it faltered? Because her words morphed from being merely true to being truly confessional. In this case, she allowed herself to confess her love, even though the confession made her seem like less of a singer.

20

LIVING IN A
CONFESSING WAY

What does it mean to confess something? We commonly think of confession as an act of acknowledging or admitting guilt or responsibility for something we have done. This is how we normally think of confession in the legal context, for example. In a Church setting, that legal definition would equate to the act of confessing some sin to an ecclesiastical leader. As important and necessary as this sometimes is, I believe that "confession" in the gospel context has a much deeper meaning than it does legally—a meaning that expands the idea of confession far beyond the kinds of confessions one might make to an ecclesiastical leader such as a bishop.

In our modern legal system, there is a presumption of innocence, and it is said that a defendant is "innocent until proven guilty." However, this is *not* the case in the gospel. As we have learned, all of us who have reached the age of accountability are guilty—guilty of *all,* in fact. This is not merely a presumption, but a fact. With respect to God, we are guilty. Always. No matter what.

To confess in the gospel sense, then, is not merely to admit to some wrong one has committed. Rather, it is to give up the charade of one's innocence—not just with respect to a particular sin but with respect to one's status before God generally. I am not at all innocent, and it is unbecoming of one who is guilty to ignore or deny or hide that fact. Unlike in the legal system, confession in the gospel is not what makes us guilty. Rather, it is what makes us honest.

Since all of us have faults and fall short of the glory of God, the scriptures teach us that we should live in what we might think of as a confessing kind of way. "Confess your faults one to another," James counsels us.[244] The phrase "one to another" implies that James is not speaking here primarily of formal ecclesiastical confessions but of a way of living openly and honestly with each other that is inherently confessional—freely apologizing, for example, or readily taking responsibility, or humbly sharing our own shortcomings and challenges when it seems appropriate and helpful to do so. This does not mean that we should go about indiscriminately speaking of our darkest sins, or standing up in testimony meetings in front of people both old and very young and revealing our most troubling thoughts. That would rarely be helpful to others. But we are ready and willing, in our interactions one with another, to admit our imperfections and struggles. We realize that innocence is not in us but in the Lord. With this understanding, we don't feel the need to hide our sins, challenges, or struggles. We similarly have no interest in, or need for, managing others' impressions of us, as our concern is not for ourselves. Like the Lord, we are content to be "of no reputation."[245] With pride neither wiring our mouths shut with respect to our sins nor compelling us to brag about our strengths and accomplishments, we are willing to speak honestly and helpfully one to another.

A sister in my stake recently told me of a comment a friend of hers made about the Church. "I could never be a Mormon," her friend told her. "You guys are all too perfect." What a tragedy it is that anyone would think this! It makes me wonder how we perhaps perpetuate this myth—the charade of our innocence—and therefore provoke disinterest or discomfort in others. The preamble to section 107 of the Doctrine and Covenants certainly gives a different view of the Church than this woman had. "The Twelve met in council," we are told, "confessing their individual weaknesses and shortcomings, expressing repentance, and seeking further guidance from the Lord." The Lord's guidance *follows* confession and repentance, even for his leaders on earth. If the Lord's apostles find it needful and helpful to speak of their weaknesses and shortcomings, how blind or hardened or seized by pride must I be if *I* don't feel the need to do so?

Describing the Sabbath, the Lord said: "But remember that on this, the Lord's day, thou shalt offer thine oblations and thy sacraments unto the Most High, confessing thy sins unto thy brethren, and before the Lord."[246] I wonder how our Sabbath experiences at Church might be different if we really applied this counsel. How would our teaching be different, for example, if we taught in a confessing way?

I remember a talk given by Elder Marlin K. Jensen in general conference years ago, when he confessed to how he found himself growing inwardly impatient for a couple of visits from old friends to end so that he could get back to writing his conference talk about friendship![247] I'll never forget that comment. Its humble honesty cut me to the quick and invited me to see the many times that I have done exactly the same kind of thing—sinning in the name of piety. He easily could have just told us to be more friendly, but his words had far greater power unto repentance precisely because they were expressions of his *own* discoveries and repentance regarding friendship.

It seems to me that teaching in a confessing way means that we would be willing to share what we have learned in our own repentant journeys. If I have been asked to speak about reverence, for example, then my text, including the scriptures, might be my own struggles and challenges regarding reverence, and how I am trying, with the Lord's help, to overcome them.

That would be a talk on reverence that no one would forget, precisely because my own honest repentance would be inviting the same in those who heard it. The same goes for a lesson on food storage or a talk on forgiveness—in most cases, the most helpful way to preach "naught but repentance"[248] is to speak of my own repentance relative to the topic I am addressing.

There is a brother in my ward from whom I relearn this point every time he speaks. He doesn't stand up as the expert whose job it is to take the rest of us to task. Rather, he stands meekly before the congregation and confesses that he is the weakest of us all and can therefore speak only in faith about what he has been asked to address. I hang on his every word because his words resonate with honesty. His confessions give voice to my own.

Likewise, how might our comments in our classes be different if we participated in a confessing way? Another brother in our ward has been my example on *this* topic. Discussions in our class, as I'm sure they do in all classes, sometimes turn to the sins of "others." A well-intentioned member, let's call him Brother Jones, may say something like this: "You know, I can't believe how some people just completely ignore the word of God and brush it off like it doesn't really matter."

Let's suppose that someone in that classroom falls into that category—a person who doesn't take the scriptures or general conference very seriously, for example. Is such a comment likely to invite them to change? Doubtful. But compare that to the comment a good friend in my neighborhood would likely make in response to such a remark. I can imagine his words with confidence because I have heard him make the following kind of statement countless times: "You know, I hear what Brother Jones is saying, and I have to say that, as I reflect upon my own life, I am definitely one of those people who too frequently undervalue or ignore the word of God. For example, I've been told for as long as I can remember that we should be reading scriptures every day as a family. But you know what, we still struggle with that—most of all because of me. If I, as the father, just stepped up more, I could be of much more help to my family. And the Church magazines—don't even get me started on that. I'm afraid I ignore the word of God as much as anybody. I need to step it up."

Now, compare those two comments. Which one invites more introspection and repentance? Which one carries the Spirit? Which one encourages us to stretch and progress? Isn't it interesting how repentant confessions of sin have much more power to invite others to repentance than do accusations of sinfulness? And think of these two brothers. Which one do you already respond to the best? Which one do you find inspiring? Which brother do you most want to emulate? Once again, isn't it the openly repentant one—the one who has given up the charade of his own innocence—whom we feel endeared to, and from whom we are likely to learn the most?

This good brother and all others like him manifest the

Lord's power in their lives and keep us in remembrance of the humble truth that each of us is fallen and unclean before the Lord. If that is true, and it is, then I have all the examples of uncleanliness that I need simply by pondering my own life. I needn't point at others to find examples of a sin that I want to decry. To teach and comment and support and live in a confessing way is to openly put myself forward as the one, perhaps most of all, who is struggling and needs to improve. It is to be meek and lowly in heart. If the Apostle Paul could characterize himself as the "least of all saints" and the "chief of all sinners,"[249] then the description surely fits me as well. As I embrace this view and begin to live more meekly and confessionally, I will find, to my surprise, that others will respond to me and to what I say much more favorably than they ever have. There is something irresistible about an unflinchingly self-honest soul—one who, like Nephi, walks "in the path of the low valley" and is content in the "plain road."[250]

Two practices describe what might be considered the secret of the meek—that is, the secret of those who "inherit the earth."[251] That secret is to simultaneously live James 5:16 and Philippians 4:8. James tells us to confess our sins one to another. As we discussed earlier, in Philippians Paul tells us to focus on anything that is virtuous or praiseworthy in others, rather than upon their sins or imperfections. This is the magic combination: Focus on our own sins and upon others' virtues.

Do this, and our teaching, our thinking, our befriending, and our parenting will all be transformed for the better.

And no one will worry that our congregations are collections of people too impressive either to listen to or to join.

21

CONFESSION'S TWIN

A friend of mine recently expressed a concern about the idea of living in a confessing way. "What of the person," he asked, "who keeps repeating the same sinful behaviors but who nevertheless is very open about what he is doing and keeps confessing his challenges and shortcomings? He is confessing his faults, I suppose, but that hardly seems sufficient."

This is an important insight. Confession alone is not sufficient, as it comes with a companion requirement. "By this ye may know if a man repenteth of his sins," the Lord declared, "behold, he will confess them and forsake them."[252] With the Lord's test in mind, let's consider my friend's implied question: What of the man who keeps confessing but also keeps repeating his sins? Has he repented? The scripture says no. We are to confess our sins and shortcomings *and* to make acceptable efforts before the Lord to forsake them. Mortality and its attendant temptations may form part of our story but can never be an excuse.

What about the other case, however—the case of one who successfully forsakes his sins but never confesses them? Has *he* repented? Interestingly, the scripture again says no. There is no true repentance without willingness to confess that sin, just as there is no true repentance without forsaking that sin. Both are necessary; neither, alone, is sufficient. But why is this the case? Why isn't simply forsaking enough?

In order to address this question, I invite you to consider a story. Years ago, when I was in high school, I had the role during a school assembly of introducing the various dress-up days that we would be having over the next week, which was Homecoming Week. We had planned Occupation Day, Sports Day, Nerd Day, School Colors Day, and Punk Rock Day. I was trying to pump up the crowd for all of the week's events, and in particular was trying to get people to want to show their school spirit by dressing up for the various days.

I described each of the first four themes and then came to our theme for Punk Rock Day. These were the days of DEVO and the emergence of punk rock from the underground. We had a relatively small but vocal group of students who were punk rock enthusiasts. One of the leaders among them was a fellow young man in my ward—a great guy and one of only a handful of LDS students in the school. "So on Punk Rock Day," I bellowed into the microphone, "those of you who are into punk rock, fantastic. Come to school dressed to the hilt—show us your enthusiasm. As for everyone else, get into it and come and show the punk rockers how stupid you think they really look!" The gymnasium erupted. I had succeeded in stoking the fire. But then I saw my friend from my ward. Tears were streaming down his cheeks.

As I sat down, I knew that I had done something terrible. I had ignited the passions of the majority against an easily targeted and essentially powerless minority. I ached. I felt bad for my friend and for *his* friends. I was embarrassed for myself. As students were filing out to their classes after the assembly, I hurried quietly out of the gym, the commotion around me barely audible as I was feeling overwhelmed by my own regrets.

What could I do? The deed was done. I had hurt my friend and had disregarded the feelings of some of my classmates. I wished that I could go back in time. Given the impossibility of that, I yearned for a hole to climb into where I could dream the whole scenario away. I felt trapped in my mistake.

My shame alone would have kept me from making the same kind of mistake again—which is to say that one can forsake a sin and never repeat it for selfish as well as for loving reasons. The act of forsaking a sin, by itself, does not cure what is sometimes called "the mother of all sins"—pride—the sin that gives birth to all other sins. Whether I forsake a sin for meek or for prideful reasons, it is only confession that assaults my sinfulness head-on. Pride cannot allow me to say, or to reveal, what the Spirit beckons me to confess. To finally say it—fully and without any vain withholding—is to render pride powerless and the cleansing Spirit of the Lord victorious.

This is why, when we finally confess, we are surprised to discover that it was not the painful thing we had imagined, but is instead liberating and joyful. How could we have been so wrong? Because when we imagine confessing, we are thinking about it from the perspective of our pride. And from that vantage point, confession is, indeed, a fatal blow—that is, to the ego. So it seems the hardest thing we could do—unbearable, perhaps even unthinkable. But when we exercise our faith and confess anyway, the pride that was protesting is obliterated. And then we discover the truth: that what seemed heavy and unbearable is the lightest thing under the heavens.

So what does this mean in the case of my public insensitivity toward the punk rock enthusiasts in my school? What kind of confession was needful? At least three: confession to God, apologies to anyone who had been harmed by what I had done, and a willingness to speak of what I had done and the challenges I had created whenever it would be appropriate and helpful to do so. Reticence to do any of these would be evidence of an ego that still hadn't let go—my need to be seen as without sin being itself a manifestation of sin.

I knew I had done wrong by God and by those I had

disparaged. I needed to come clean. So I went into the principal's office and requested to use the school intercom system to make a public apology during the class period immediately following the assembly. I don't remember what I said, but it was a heartfelt attempt to undo the harm I had done. I walked out of that office a different and lighter person, a confessing heart having been added to my soul's commitment to forsake that kind of insensitivity in the future.

My public apology did one additional thing in this case—something else that is essential to the confessional life. The offense was young enough that the public confession ended up being an act of restitution as well. But it might not have turned out that way. My comments could have created such a terrible burden that one meager apology couldn't have begun to heal the wounds. Others might have still struggled even if I no longer struggled myself. As we will explore in the next chapter, in such cases my work is not finished. We repent of our sins in part by continuing to help those who might still be burdened by them.

22

TOWARD RECONCILIATION

If ye shall come unto me, or shall desire to come unto me," the Lord taught, "and rememberest that thy brother hath aught against thee—Go thy way unto thy brother, and first be reconciled to thy brother, and then come unto me with full purpose of heart, and I will receive you."[253]

Here the Savior declares two bold truths. First, our reconciliation with God depends on our reconciliation with each other. *If you want me to receive you,* he is saying, *then you must first receive each other.* In order to understand the second truth, we first need to see what the Lord *isn't* saying in this passage. He is not merely saying that we have a duty to go become reconciled with others if *we* have something against *them,* but that we have an obligation to go to them and facilitate reconciliation if *they* have something against *us*. This is evidently true even if we ourselves don't have any hard feelings at all!

This is the very heart of the confessional life. We remain open to and regretful about any difficulties we might have caused others, even if we ourselves have long since forsaken the actions or feelings that originally added to them. If others still struggle, we don't minimize their challenges or tell them to get over it. Spouses who have been unfaithful, for example, do not become embittered at mates who are still struggling over it, even if many years later. They might know that it would be better for their mates' well-being if they were able to let it go, but they would never blame them if they couldn't. The offending spouses would do everything they could do to carry the burden they had helped to create, for as long as that burden needed to be carried. Likewise, spouses who had remained faithful, upon awakening to the burden that their long struggles to forgive had caused for their mates, would then set about to carry *those* burdens as long as they needed to be carried.

This is the spirit of restitution and the pathway to reconciliation. We don't tell ourselves that others are guilty and we are not. Rather, whatever the other may be struggling with reminds us of struggles of our own—whether in this area of our lives or in some other. If they are struggling with us, we understand that too. We come to them having given up the charade of our own innocence—our own apologetic and confessional ways being more helpful than anything else we could ever do.

A dear friend once extended a most gracious hand of fellowship and reconciliation to me. We had been estranged for a few years, and I was still struggling with something. The fact that he himself was no longer struggling did not keep him from reaching out to me. He was living the Savior's teaching, and I was the beneficiary. I still have his letter, and I still wish that I had not sent my reply.

Have you ever sent a note you wish you hadn't? This particular letter is the one I regret most. My words hurt him. How could they not have? He flinched but did not take offense as he easily could have. He was still there for me in a way that helped me to finally come to my senses. My words were forgotten; he did not hold them over me. His gift to me awakened me to the restitution that I then owed him. Like a sliver festering under the skin, what we have been holding back needs to be released. In my case, I still had a book that I had borrowed from him many years earlier. Or at least that was the story I had long told myself. Under the light of his love, however, I finally could no longer deny the truth: I hadn't borrowed the book, I had stolen it. I had taken it to read for myself when he himself needed it. I never asked him for it, and I never told him that I had it. I had stolen it then, and I had continued stealing it for all the years since. My claim of righteousness had not allowed me to see my sin. So I returned his book, together with a long overdue apology.

When we begin to live confessionally, we feel the obligation and desire to make others as whole as they can be made from the trouble we have caused them. Nothing they have done to us can hold us back from making restitution ourselves. Of course, it is the nature of sins that, once committed, mortals cannot fully atone for them. The deep scars we inflict on one another can be reached only by the One who has healing in his wings.[254] But this doesn't absolve us from doing all that we imperfectly can do. It simply binds us to the Savior, as one of the instruments in his hands.

23

DIVINE REBUKE

I remember a basketball practice years ago when our coach absolutely tore into a few of us on the team. I don't remember anymore what his specific complaints were, but I remember what he said to us at the end of practice that day. "Don't worry if I get after you," he told us. "That just means I believe in you—that I know you can be better. The time you should begin worrying is when I'm no longer getting after you, because that would mean that I have given up on you." So it is, I believe, with God.

Except that God doesn't give up.

"Happy is the man whom God correcteth," the scriptures tell us.[255] "For whom the Lord loveth he correcteth; even as a father the son in whom he delighteth."[256] The Lord repeated this truth to John in the book of Revelation when he said, "As many as I love, I rebuke and chasten: be zealous therefore, and repent."[237]

The Lord awakens us to our faults precisely *because* he loves us and wants us to be with him and to be like him—to enjoy the kind of life that he enjoys: eternal life. This explains in part why many of those whom we revere in the scriptures also struggled mightily with their personal challenges. Enoch lamented that his lack of talent caused all the people (not just some, but *all*) to hate him.[258] Moses likewise felt inadequate because of his lack of eloquence and his "slow tongue."[259] Martha felt burdened by all she had to do.[260] Peter wept bitterly after realizing he had denied for the third time that he knew Jesus.[261] Nephi felt that he was a wretched person because of his iniquities.[262] Enos was filled with guilt and worry for his own soul.[263] Zeezrom was so troubled by his sins that he lay with a burning fever, finding no deliverance.[264] Leah struggled with not being loved.[265] Paul was burdened by an unnamed challenge that weighed him down[266] and lamented his wretchedness and carnal nature.[267] Rachel's distress at not being able to bear children was so great that she longed to die.[268] Jonah's soul fainted within him because of his sins and predicament.[269] Joseph Smith lamented that he frequently fell into many foolish errors and temptations, offensive in the sight of God.[270] The widow of Zarephath had exhausted all her resources and was resigned to starving to death with her son.[271] Alma was haunted by all of his sins and iniquities and tormented with the pains of hell.[272]

The Lord did not rush in to rescue these people from their struggles. His love for them, and for us, dictated that he didn't—and doesn't. Faith is forged when one's back is against the wall. When we finally realize that no strength of this world—our own, most of all—can rescue us from our fate, then we feel keenly both our predicament and the Lord's redeeming grace. "The Lord is not slack concerning his promise, as some men count slackness," Peter assured us, "but is longsuffering to us-ward, not willing that any should perish, but that all should come to repentance."[273] Part of the Lord's love is his forbearance from rescuing us from the challenges and heartaches that will lead us to further repentance if we will let them. This is not slackness toward us, but long-suffering love.

In just the same way, God's chastisements and rebukes of us are part of his longsuffering as well. "Where sin abound[s]," Paul taught, grace must abound toward us even more.[274] And part of that grace which abounds toward us is manifested through the rebukes of a loving Parent to children who are not yet seeing what they must see if they are ever to be able to return. This is the message that came to me during the flight on the plane that I mentioned in chapter 11, a message that has been repeated to me through other experiences many times before and since. When we approach the divine, we are overwhelmed both by God's love and by our own weakness. Actually, this comes in reverse. It is precisely because his presence makes our own unworthiness obvious that the love we feel from him is so overwhelming. *How could he love such a one as me?* we exclaim in disbelief. But he does. *Doesn't he know what I've done?* Yes, he knows it better than we do. *Then how can he still love me?* Because love is who he is. If he didn't love us despite all, he would not be God. A friend of mine often says, "God doesn't love us because we are good, he loves us because he is good." And so it is.

Another friend told me this story. He was grading his students' finals in his university office when he became disturbed by an odd kind of noise outside of his office door. It sounded a bit like someone was rustling some papers out in the hallway. He tried to ignore the sound until, after about five minutes, he could take it no longer. He left his task, walked over to the door, and opened it. The sound had not been rustling papers. There at his door stood one of his students. She was hyperventilating out of fear. He invited her in and tried to calm her. Through tears, she confessed something that, in her mind, threatened all that she had ever hoped for.

"A week ago," the student said, "you sent an e-mail to me saying that I had failed to turn in an assignment that was a substantial part of my grade. I e-mailed you back, saying that I had e-mailed it to you two days earlier."

The professor nodded. "Yes, I remember. I get tons of e-mails and miss them all the time. I apologized, and you re-sent me your assignment."

The student began shaking violently, and tears streamed down her cheeks. "Yes, but it was a lie. I hadn't sent it to you at all, I just said that I had. I was afraid that you would fail me because I had missed the deadline!" She cried even harder. "And now I'll fail for sure because I lied!"

It turns out that this young student was anxious about much more than her grade in the class. She was afraid that she had disqualified herself even from the right and ability to graduate. In her mind, her dishonesty was a sin that this institution of higher learning could not countenance. She was confessing to something that she thought would ruin her.

When my friend told me this story, my heart was overwhelmed with love for this meek and courageous young student, just as my friend's was when he received the confession. I was struck, as well, by how powerful a metaphor this story is for life. It is so easy, isn't it, to spiritually hyperventilate ourselves to the point that we believe that any one sin puts our eternity at risk. But in our gasping for breath, we are forgetting the Savior. He knew we would fail. He knew we would transgress. His plan contains the solution for this. He paid for our sins because he knew we would commit them! He doesn't love us less for having committed them. Forgiveness awaits if we but come to him. And sanctification is promised if we continue to repentantly cling to the rod and allow his Spirit to change us. On the one hand, we are separated from him by every sin. On the other hand, this separation is what by necessity binds us to him. We need not despair.

Whatever grade this student ended up receiving meant nothing in comparison to the lesson she allowed herself to learn: that the most exquisite joy is felt only when we listen to and act upon the Lord's whispered rebukes. He loves us so much that if we don't heed the whisperings, he will find ways to shout to us—some way to reach our hardened souls. Whatever his tone of communication, his chastisement is the love we have been waiting for, and in our listening to that chastisement we will finally find the happiness that we have been consumed with obtaining but that has always seemed just beyond our grasp.

The truth is, this happiness has never been "just" beyond our grasp at all, but a million light years beyond it. It exists only in *His* grasp. Everything that has kept us from him, including our resistance to the rebukes we need to hear, has been keeping us from *it*.

This is a realization that brings me to a dream I had many years ago. The scriptures speak of both dreams and visions, sometimes blurring the line between them. In this particular case, what I saw was definitely a dream and not any kind of vision. It hinted at something I believe we all may experience one day. I hope, however, when that day comes for me, that the experience will end differently than it did in my dream. For I learned that I wasn't yet prepared for what is to come.

2 4

FINALLY FALLING

Years ago I dreamed that my father and I were together in an elevator. We were alone and rode in silence. I don't recall much about the ride except that we were ascending. I didn't know where we were going or why, yet I had the overwhelming impression that this was a very important trip. For some reason that I could not articulate, it also seemed clear to me that my father *did* know the reason for our trip as well as our destination. It seemed a journey he had already experienced, and that he accompanied me on this trip as my escort.

After a long while, the elevator came to a stop. As the doors opened, I recall being overcome by the presence of an incredible being. Words fail me here. This being radiated a light that was bright beyond my capacity to describe or imagine.

He turned toward me the moment the doors opened, and it seemed that he had been waiting specifically for me. He exuded a warmth and love that attracted me to him immediately. I rushed to him and we embraced. I felt an indescribable love, and I remember realizing at once that this must be my Savior, Jesus Christ.

But I shudder when I think of what happened next. I remember wondering, while in the Lord's embrace, whether it was really him. On the one hand, I knew—his arms were around me; I had been enveloped in his love. On the other hand, I somehow *didn't* know. Something in the way I had been living my life was holding me back from a fulness. At that very moment of exquisite joy and excruciating doubt, I awoke.

As I lay in wonder upon my bed, I was overwhelmed by what I had just seen and still felt. *Why hadn't I known for sure?* The question both haunted and inspired me. I believed that the embrace I had experienced was a foreshadowing of an embrace that yet awaited me. It seemed that I might have been allowed to experience a representation of it because I wasn't yet ready for what was to come. The dream was at once an offering of the most divine love I had ever experienced and the most scathing rebuke I had ever received. It seemed that out of love for me, God had awakened me more fully to my sinfulness. I had been invited to a deeper and more complete repentance. He had beckoned me, as Lehi did his sons, to partake of the fruit of his love—a gift I could receive only by grabbing more tightly to the rod and allowing it to take me more deeply along the strait and narrow path of repentance.

As I reflect now upon this dream, I am stunned by something I am seeing for the first time as I write these words—a detail I had never noticed, a truth that is just now penetrating me. *I didn't fall at his feet!*

This is the answer that I have long sought! Perhaps I couldn't know him for sure because every particle of my soul had not yet learned or felt compelled to bow before him. What audacity simply to run to his arms, as if he were merely a friend long unseen! And yet his grace is so great that he lovingly received me even though my impetuous act revealed that I didn't really get it yet. This was my Savior and my Redeemer! This was the One who had borne all my griefs, my sorrows, and my sins! This was he who was crucified so that I might live! This was the One who had trod the winepress alone! This was my God and my King!

And yet I didn't fall before him.

Like the group in Lehi's dream that had fallen away, I had reached up to partake of the fruit. The gospel hadn't yet penetrated my soul. Not really. I didn't yet understand that it was all a gift: the path, the rod, the tree, the fruit—all had been placed before me by him! In fact, he was himself the gift. He, himself, is the path, or "the way."[275] He, himself, is the rod, or "the word."[276] He, himself, is the Tree of Life.[277] He, himself, is the first fruits or "the love of God."[278] Every saving element in Lehi's dream is a representation of Christ himself, each element capturing a facet of his saving offering to me and to us.

And yet I didn't fall.

I pray to God that when one day I have the blessing of that sacred meeting, I will know his divinity and my nothingness enough that I will be able to do nothing but crumble in gratitude before him. Then, when he lifts me, I will know. I will finally understand all that my pride has kept me from. Any need to love myself or to approve of myself or to think well of myself will finally and fully be melted away by the realization that he loves me despite all I have done and been. My smallness will be swallowed up by his wholeness, my self-concern consumed by his selfless love.

> And behold, a woman in the city, which was a sinner, when she knew that Jesus sat at meat in the Pharisee's house, brought an alabaster box of ointment, and stood at his feet behind him weeping, and began to wash his feet with tears, and did wipe them with the hairs of her head, and kissed his feet, and anointed them with the ointment.
>
> Now when the Pharisee . . . saw it, he spake within himself, saying, This man, if he were a prophet, would have known who and what manner of woman this is that toucheth him: for she is a sinner.
>
> And Jesus . . . said unto [him], Seest thou this

woman? I entered into thine house, thou gavest me no water for my feet: but she hath washed my feet with tears, and wiped them with the hairs of her head. Thou gavest me no kiss: but this woman since the time I came in hath not ceased to kiss my feet. My head with oil thou didst not anoint: but this woman hath anointed my feet with ointment. Wherefore I say unto thee, Her sins, which are many, are forgiven; for she has loved much: but to whom little is forgiven, the same loveth little.

And he said unto her, Thy sins are forgiven.[279]

This woman knew who Jesus was, and she knew who she was relative to him. She wept and bowed and fell at his feet. Others mocked, but it mattered not. Still she fell down and partook of the fruit of happiness.[280]

"Knowest thou the meaning of the tree?" the angel asked Nephi when he was shown what his father had seen.[281] In answer, Nephi was granted a vision where he "saw many fall down at [the] feet [of the Son of God] and worship him."[282] Who can understand? Up is down and down is up, so long as we are down before the Lord. The fall that brought hardship and heartache into the world is overcome within us as we choose voluntarily to fall again—this time before Christ.

So long as we insist on reaching up, our hearts and souls will never be lifted. If, on the other hand, we fall humbly and repentantly before him, we will never be down. This is the divine and surprising truth that unlocks for us the happiness that can seem so elusive.

Happiness, like heaven, may seem above us, but it turns out that we find both of them by falling.

NOTES

1. See Matthew 22:39.

2. See 1 Samuel 18:1–4.

3. Mosiah 18:21. See also 1 Samuel 18:1.

4. Hebrews 13:3.

5. 2 Timothy 3:2.

6. See Luke 17:33.

7. D&C 19:21. See also D&C 6:9; 11:9.

8. Ether 12:27.

9. See Mosiah 3:19.

10. Matthew 11:28.

11. Matthew 11:29–30.

12. See Matthew 11:28–30.

13. See Matthew 16:25.

14. See Matthew 11:29–30.

15. Matthew 10:39.

16. Mark 10:44.

17. 1 Corinthians 3:18.

18. 2 Corinthians 12:10.

19. 1 Nephi 12:10; emphasis added.

20. Isaiah 53:5; emphasis added.

21. Dieter F. Uchtdorf, "You Matter to Him," *Ensign,* November 2011, 20.

22. See Moses 1:10; Mosiah 4:1–3.

23. See Mosiah 3:19.

24. See 1 Nephi 8:10, 12.

25. See 1 Nephi 8. See also 1 Nephi 11–15.

26. See 1 Nephi 8:26–27.

27. See 1 Nephi 8:27.

28. See 1 Nephi 11:34–35.

29. See 1 Nephi 12:18.

30. See 1 Nephi 8:20–21.

31. See 1 Nephi 8:21.

32. See 1 Nephi 8:23.

33. See 1 Nephi 12:17.

34. See 1 Nephi 11:25.

35. See 1 Nephi 8:24.

36. 1 Nephi 8:25.

37. See 1 Nephi 8:28.

38. 1 Nephi 8:30.

39. See 1 Nephi 8:26.

40. See 1 Nephi 11:36.

41. See Alma 30:6.

42. Alma 30:13; emphasis added.

43. See Alma 30:23; emphasis added.

44. Alma 30:23, 27; emphasis added.

45. Alma 30:18; emphasis added.

46. See Alma 30:17.

47. See Alma 30:16.

48. See Alma 30:53.

49. See Alma 30:18.

50. See Alma 30:59–60; emphasis added.

51. Alma 31:13.

52. See Alma 31:21.

53. Alma 31:16–18.

54. See Alma 31:19.

55. Alma 31:27.

56. Luke 17:33.

57. See Alma 32:2.

58. See Alma 32:5.

59. Alma 32:8.

60. Alma 32:13.

61. Neal A. Maxwell, *Deposition of a Disciple* (Salt Lake City: Deseret Book, 1976), 29.

62. Matthew 11:30.

63. See Ether 12:27.

64. Moses 1:10.

65. C. S. Lewis, *The Last*

Battle (New York: HarperCollins, 1956), 188–89.

66. 3 Nephi 12:3; emphasis added.

67. See Alma 32:42.

68. See Alma 30:17, 23, 27.

69. See Moroni 7:41–42.

70. Alma 32:21.

71. See Alma 32:27–43.

72. See Alma 32:41.

73. See Alma 32:28.

74. See Alma 31:16–17.

75. See John 1:1.

76. See Alma 32:27.

77. See Alma 33:1.

78. Alma 33:10–11.

79. Alma 33:16.

80. Alma 33:22–23; emphasis added.

81. D&C 88:6.

82. See 1 Nephi 19:9; 2 Nephi 9:21; Alma 7:11.

83. See 1 Nephi 8:10, 12.

84. See 1 Nephi 8:10–12.

85. See Alma 32:13.

86. See Matthew 20:1–16.

87. See Luke 15:11–32.

88. See Luke 10:30–37.

89. See Mark 9:34–35.

90. James 2:10.

91. Romans 3:19.

92. See Romans 3:27.

93. See 2 Nephi 31:19.

94. See Luke 7:41–43.

95. See D&C 93:36.

96. See, for example, D&C 20:30–31.

97. See Psalm 24:4.

98. D&C 88:18.

99. D&C 88:22; emphasis added.

100. See Moroni 7:48.

101. See, for example, Mosiah 5:2.

102. See Helaman 10:5.

103. See 2 Nephi 2:13. See also Alma 42:13, 17–18.

104. Mosiah 5:2.

105. 2 Nephi 2:8.

106. See 2 Nephi 9:53; Jacob 4:7.

107. See 2 Nephi 33:6.

108. See D&C 60:7.

NOTES

109. Brigham Young, in *Journal of Discourses,* 26 vols. (London: Latter-day Saints Book Depot, 1854–86), 3:47.
110. See Alma 30:13–27.
111. See John 1:16; Helaman 12:24; D&C 93:20.
112. Numbers 21:6.
113. See Numbers 21:7.
114. See Numbers 21:7–9.
115. John 3:14–15. See also Alma 33:19.
116. See D&C 84:27; Hebrews 7:16.
117. Hebrews 10:4.
118. See Hebrews 10:1–2.
119. 3 Nephi 15:4, 8.
120. See 3 Nephi 15:9–10; emphasis added.
121. John 14:15; emphasis added.
122. See 3 Nephi 12:21–22.
123. 3 Nephi 12:27–29; emphasis added.
124. 3 Nephi 12:5.
125. 3 Nephi 12:7.
126. 3 Nephi 12:8.
127. D&C 121:45.
128. See John 15:12.
129. See D&C 88:22.
130. See Moroni 10:33.
131. Alma 57:21; emphasis added.
132. 3 Nephi 27:20–21.
133. 3 Nephi 12:19.
134. 3 Nephi 9:20, 22.
135. See 2 Nephi 28:21.
136. See Romans 3:23–31.
137. See Luke 10:38–42.
138. See Luke 10:40–41.
139. See Matthew 25:14–30.
140. See Matthew 25:24.
141. Matthew 25:21, 23.
142. Matthew 25:26–29.
143. See Matthew 23:23.
144. Matthew 23:28.
145. Matthew 23:26.
146. See Alma 42:16.
147. See Mosiah 24:13–14.
148. Alma 13:30.
149. D. Todd Christofferson, "The Divine Gift of Repentance," *Ensign,* November 2011, 38–41.

NOTES

150. 2 Timothy 2:25; emphasis added.

151. See 2 Nephi 31:9, 17–21.

152. See Mosiah 26:22; Alma 6:2; 7:14; 9:27; 48:19; Helaman 3:24; 5:17,19; 3 Nephi 7:26; D&C 55:2.

153. Matthew 3:11.

154. Mark 1:4.

155. See 1 Nephi 8:26–27.

156. See 1 Nephi 8:26, in which the great and spacious building floats, as it were, "in the air, high above the earth."

157. See 1 Nephi 11:36.

158. See 2 Nephi 31:20.

159. See 2 Nephi 31:21.

160. James 4:9–10.

161. See 3 Nephi 11:22.

162. 3 Nephi 11:28–29.

163. See D&C 50:17–18.

164. See D&C 64:22.

165. Moroni 7:6–9.

166. Matthew 6:2–3.

167. G. K. Chesterton, *Orthodoxy* (Chicago: Moody Publishers, 2009), 36.

168. See Matthew 23:23.

169. See 1 Samuel 16:7.

170. See Romans 3:19, 23, 27.

171. James 2:9.

172. James 2:13.

173. Matthew 9:10–13.

174. See Matthew 3:9; Luke 3:7–8; John 8:35–58.

175. See Matthew 4:18–22; 9:9; 10:2–4; Acts 9:1–6.

176. See Luke 10:30–37.

177. See Mark 12:41–44.

178. 1 Corinthians 1:27–28.

179. See 1 Corinthians 1:29–31.

180 Moroni 7:16.

181. Moroni 7:18.

182. Alma 38:14.

183. See Philippians 2:12.

184. Luke 3:5.

185. John 15:5.

186. 1 Nephi 15:8–9.

187. See 2 Nephi 26:25.

188. See Matthew 22:39.

189. See D&C 64:8–10.

190. Matthew 6:9–13.

191. Matthew 6:12; emphasis added.

192. Matthew 6:14–15.

193. James 2:13.

194. See James 2:14.

195. James 2:17.

196. John 8:11.

197. Matthew 14:31.

198. See Matthew 26:34.

199. See Matthew 26:75.

200. See Mosiah 27:11–19; Alma 36:6–21.

201. See Mosiah 4:1–3.

202. See D&C 64:10.

203. See Moroni 8:26.

204. 2 Nephi 4:17–19.

205. 2 Nephi 4:26–29.

206. 2 Nephi 4:30–33; emphasis added.

207. 2 Nephi 4:34.

208. John 8:4–5.

209. John 8:7.

210. See Moroni 10:34.

211. See John 8:10–11.

212. See 1 John 2:1; D&C 29:5; 32:3.

213. See Alma 24:10.

214. Luke 23:43.

215. See Philippians 1:13–14.

216. Philippians 4:11.

217. See Matthew 5:39–42.

218. See 2 Nephi 5:1–6.

219. See 2 Nephi 4:16–35.

220. Philippians 4:7.

221. Philippians 4:8; emphasis added.

222. Philippians 4:9.

223. 2 Nephi 4:17–19.

224. See 2 Nephi 4:27–29.

225. See Alma 36; 38.

226. Mosiah 27:35; emphasis added.

227. Alma 36:14.

228. Alma 10:5–6.

229. See Alma 10:4.

230. Mark 9:23.

231. Mark 9:24.

232. Mark 9:27.

233. See Alma 24:3.

234. See Alma 24:20.

235. Alma 24:8–10.

236. See Alma 24:11–17.

237. See Alma 24:18–19.

238. Romans 7:18–19.

239. 1 Corinthians 15:9.

240. See Ephesians 3:8.

241. 1 Timothy 1:15; emphasis added.
242. 1 Timothy 1:16.
243. See Moroni 8:26.
244. James 5:16.
245. See Philippians 2:7.
246. D&C 59:12.
247. Marlin K. Jensen, "Friendship: A Gospel Principle," *Ensign*, May 1999, 64.
248. See D&C 19:21.
249. See Ephesians 3:8; 1 Timothy 1:15.
250. See 2 Nephi 4:32.
251. See 3 Nephi 12:5.
252. D&C 58:43.
253. 3 Nephi 12:23–24.
254. See Malachi 4:2.
255. Job 5:17.
256. Proverbs 3:12.
257. Revelation 3:19.
258. See Moses 6:31.
259. See Exodus 4:10.
260. See Luke 10:40.
261. See Matthew 26:75.
262. See 2 Nephi 4:17.
263. See Enos 1:4–6.
264. See Alma 15:3.
265. See Genesis 29:31.
266. See 2 Corinthians 12:7–9.
267. See Romans 7:14–24.
268. See Genesis 30:1.
269. See Jonah 2:5–7.
270. See Joseph Smith–History 1:28.
271. See 1 Kings 17:12.
272. See Alma 36:12–13.
273. 2 Peter 3:9.
274. See Romans 5:20; Ephesians 1:8.
275. See John 14:6.
276. See 1 Nephi 11:25; John 1:1–14.
277. See Proverbs 11:30; Acts 5:30; Galatians 3:13; 1 Peter 2:24; 1 Nephi 11:21–24.
278. See 1 Corinthians 15:23; 2 Nephi 2:9; John 3:16.
279. Luke 7:37–48.
280. See 1 Nephi 8:30.
281. See 1 Nephi 11:21.
282. See 1 Nephi 11:24.

INDEX

INDEX

INDEX

God: love of, 11–12, 95–96, 167–68; and divine discontent, 25–26; separation from, 43–48; presence of, 51–53; glorying in, 97–98

Gospel: paradoxes in, 11–12, 15–16; and turning to Christ, 49–55; Brigham Young on, 54; pride and, 70; levels of focus on, 83–86. *See also* Church of Jesus Christ of Latter-day Saints

Grudges, 111–16

Guilt: importance of, 37; as mercy, 41–48; awareness of, 61–62; repentance and, 74; and self-forgiveness, 125–26; admitting, 148–49, 154

Healing, 142–43

Heart, intent and, 83–86

High school assembly, 157–60

Hinckley, Gordon B., 108

Holy Ghost, 83, 132–33

Honesty, 139–47, 168–69

Hope, 30–37

"How Great Thou Art," 147

Humiliation, 64–66

Humility, 15–16, 24–29, 32, 63–70

Inadequacy, feelings of, 64–67

Inferiority, 105–6

Innocence, 148–50

Intent, 83–86

Israelites, 58–59

Jensen, Marlin K., 151

Jesus Christ: love of, ix–x; finding happiness in, 6–8, 27–29; Alma's teachings on, 32–35; need for, 48; turning to, 49–55, 60–61; law fulfilled in, 59–60; equality in, 100–101; healing performed by, 142–43; author's dream of, 172–74; worshipping, 174–77. *See also* Atonement

Jonathan, x

Judging others, 87–93

Junior high, bullying in, 22–23

Justice, 48, 49–51

Justification, 51–53, 67

Korihor, 17–19

The Last Battle (Lewis), 28

Law, 52–53, 60–61, 75–76

INDEX

Redemption, 53, 67, 101

Remission, 75

Repentance: freedom following, 35–37; willingness in, 45, 53–54; and higher law, 61–62; as path to happiness, 71–78; from withholding love, 116–18; versus forgiving ourselves, 120–26; and confession of sins, 146–47; and living in confessing way, 150–54; repetition of sins and, 156–60; and divine rebuke, 165–71. *See also* Confession; Forgiveness; Reconciliation

Resentment, 111–16

Righteousness, 60–61, 67–69, 82–83

Sabbath, 151

Sacrament gem, 64–66

Sanctification, 51–54, 61, 74–75

Savior, need for, 48

Seed, faith compared to, 31–35

Self, love of, ix–xi

Self-concern, 70

Self-esteem, 17–21

Self-forgiveness, 119–26

Serpent of brass, 58

Service, 83–86, 87–89

Sin: and separation from God, 43–48; awareness of, 61–62; acceptable and unacceptable, 87–93; withholding love as, 116–18; admission of weaknesses and, 139–47; forsaking and repeating, 156–60; and reconciliation, 161–64; and divine rebuke, 165–71

Sinking boat, analogy of, 43–45

"Smokey Mountain," 95–96

Spiritual exceptionalism. *See* Superiority

Student, confession of, 168–69

Suffering, 96

Superiority: and acceptable and unacceptable sins, 87–93; by association, 94–99; by nature, 100–109

Support, during trials, 77

Talents, parable of, 69–70

Teaching, in confessing way, 151–54

Teasing, 22–23

Teenagers, help author on highway, 87–89